BRAIN QUEST

GRADE 3
WORKBOOK

Written by Jan Meyer
Consulting Editor: Anna Shults

Workman Publishing • New York

This book belongs to:

ISBN 978-1-5235-1737-4

New and updated text by Jen Agresta and Jennifer Szymanski; educational review by Anne Haywood, Peg Keiner, and Rebecca Keller

Illustrations by Kimble Mead and Scott Dubar, with cover illustrations by Edison Yan

Workbook series design by Raquel Jaramillo

30th Anniversary Edition Revision produced for Workman by WonderLab Group, LLC, and Fan Works Design, LLC.

Workman books are available at special discounts when purchased in bulk for premiums and sales promotions as well as for fundraising or educational use. Special editions or book excerpts can also be created to specification. For details, please contact special.markets@hbgusa.com.

WORKMAN, BRAIN QUEST, and IT'S FUN TO BE SMART! are registered trademarks of Workman Publishing Co., Inc., a subsidiary of Hachette Book Group, Inc.

Workman Publishing Co., Inc.,
a subsidiary of Hachette Book Group, Inc.
1290 Avenue of the Americas
New York, NY 10104
workman.com • brainquest.com

Distributed in Europe by Hachette Livre, 58 rue Jean Bleuzen, 92 178 Vanves Cedex, France.

Distributed in the United Kingdom by Hachette Book Group, UK, Carmelite House, 50 Victoria Embankment, London EC4Y 0DZ.

Printed in the USA on responsibly sourced paper.

First printing April 2023
10 9 8 7 6 5 4 3 2 1

Dear Parents and Caregivers,

Learning is an adventure—a quest for knowledge. At Brain Quest, we strive to guide children on that quest, to keep them motivated and curious, and to give them the confidence they need to do well in school and beyond. We're excited to partner with you and your child on this step of their lifelong knowledge quest.

BRAIN QUEST WORKBOOKS are designed to enrich children's understandings in all content areas by reinforcing the basics and previewing future learning. These are not textbooks, but rather true workbooks, and are best used to reinforce curricular concepts learned at school. Each workbook aligns with national and state learning standards and is written in consultation with an award-winning grade-level teacher.

In third grade, children extend their reading and vocabulary skills in language arts, math, science, and social studies. They broaden their writing skills, regularly writing paragraphs in reports and projects. They connect fractions to decimals and practice computation, rounding, and estimating. Third graders begin to apply these skills to real world examples through problem-solving.

We're excited that BRAIN QUEST WORKBOOKS will play an integral role in your child's educational adventure. So, let the learning—and the fun—begin!

It's fun to be smart!®

—The editors of Brain Quest

HOW TO USE THIS BOOK

Welcome to the Brain Quest Grade 3 Workbook!

Encourage your child to complete the workbook at their own pace. Guide them to approach the work with a **growth mindset**, the idea that our abilities can change and grow with effort. Reinforce this by praising effort and problem-solving and explaining that mistakes are part of learning.

The **opening page** of each section has a note for parents and caregivers and another note just for kids.

81

READING

Do you prefer reading fiction or nonfiction? Do you have a favorite genre? I like reading myths, fairy tales, biographies, and books about history. Let's check out the different kinds of texts in this section!

PARENTS In this section, your child will practice key reading comprehension skills: cause and effect, sequencing, identifying key ideas and details, and more. Developing these skills gives learners the tools they need to be independent and enthusiastic readers.

For additional resources, visit www.BrainQuest.com/grade3

PLACE A STICKER HERE

Notes to children give learners a preview of each section.

Notes to parents highlight key skills and give suggestions for helping with each section.

Guide your child to place a sticker here to get excited about learning.

Read the directions aloud if needed. Encourage your child to work as independently as possible.

Get your child talking! Ask about the images they see and connections between the workbook and their lives.

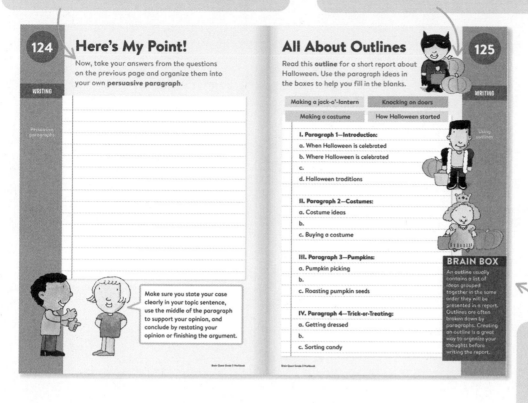

124

WRITING

Persuasive paragraphs

Here's My Point!

Now, take your answers from the questions on the previous page and organize them into your own **persuasive paragraph**.

Make sure you state your case clearly in your topic sentence, use the middle of the paragraph to support your opinion, and conclude by restating your opinion or finishing the argument.

Brain Quest Grade 3 Workbook

All About Outlines

Read this **outline** for a short report about Halloween. Use the paragraph ideas in the boxes to help you fill in the blanks.

125

WRITING

Using outlines

| Making a jack-o'-lantern | Knocking on doors |
| Making a costume | How Halloween started |

I. Paragraph 1—Introduction:
a. When Halloween is celebrated
b. Where Halloween is celebrated
c.
d. Halloween traditions

II. Paragraph 2—Costumes:
a. Costume ideas
b.
c. Buying a costume

III. Paragraph 3—Pumpkins:
a. Pumpkin picking
b.
c. Roasting pumpkin seeds

IV. Paragraph 4—Trick-or-Treating:
a. Getting dressed
b.
c. Sorting candy

BRAIN BOX

An outline usually contains a list of ideas grouped together in the same order they will be presented in a report. Outlines are often broken down by paragraphs. Creating an outline is a great way to organize your thoughts before writing the report.

Brain Quest Grade 3 Workbook

Brain Boxes offer friendly explanations of key concepts.

Cut out the Brain Quest **Mini-Deck** from the back to play and learn on the go!

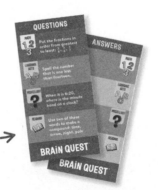

After each chapter, have your child place a sticker on the **progress map** to mark their achievement.

Encourage your child to use stickers to decorate the **certificate.** Hang it up when it's complete!

CERTIFICATE OF
ACHIEVEMENT
Earned by

for completing all sections in the
BRAIN QUEST
GRADE 3 WORKBOOK

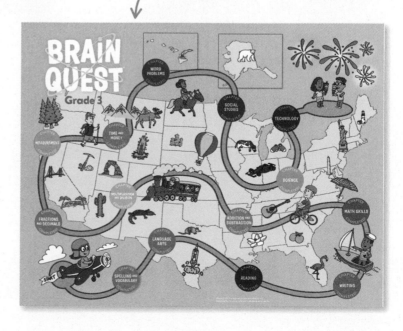

CONTENTS

SPELLING AND VOCABULARY

Adding letters to the beginning of a word (a prefix) or the end of a word (a suffix) can be the difference between something ordinary and something *extra*ordinary. Let's *up*grade our spelling and vocabulary skills!

PARENTS Learning about prefixes, suffixes, and root words unlocks a deeper understanding of the English language. In this section, your child will practice regular and irregular word spellings, prefixes and suffixes, antonyms and synonyms, dictionary skills, and more.

PLACE A STICKER HERE

The Long and Short of It

Circle the correct spelling of the **long vowel** word. Then sort the words by spelling pattern on the cards below.

Molly gave a bath to the straigh (stray) straye dog.

Reid wanted extra cheese chease chese on his pizza.

Mackenzie put her music museic mussic notebook in her toat tote tot bag.

It was a good day to take the bote boat out on the lake laik layk .

Shonda got in lin line lyn to see the rhino rhighno rhyno .

The school should suppli suppligh supply the chalk.

Most of the artists painted paynted on eesels easels .

Gavin used uesed the key kee kea to open oapen his huge hug heug art studio.

Eight Eaght Ait little ducklings crossed the pathway.

The waitress took a coffee break braik brayk .

---

long a words
stray
_____
_____
_____
_____
The long a sound can be spelled:
a_e, ai, ay, ea, or ei

long e words
_____
_____
_____
The long e sound can be spelled:
ee, ea, or ey

long i words
_____
_____
The long i sound can be spelled:
i, i_e, or y

long o words
_____
_____
_____
The long o sound can be spelled:
o, o_e, or oa

long u words
_____
_____
_____
The long u sound can be spelled:
u, u_e, or ue

Circle the correct spelling of the **short vowel** word. Then sort the words by spelling pattern on the cards below.

The new girl at school made frends friends quickly.

Ebony called ahead ahed to make a reservation.

Jung left his ombrella umbrella on the bus bos .

Katherine stepped onto the bottom botom bohtom rung of the read red raid ladder.

The audience laffed laughed at all the funny things the actors sed said sead .

He grabbed graibbed his skates and went down to the roller renk rink rynk.

The little pig pyg is bright pynk penk pink .

Dylan put a sauddle saeddle saddle on the horse.

Jenna ordered turkey and ham on rye bred bread .

Raquel needed to wash wosh her bicycle.

short a words
_____
_____
_____
The short a sound can be spelled: au or a

short o words
_____
_____
_____
The short o sound is usually spelled: o or a

short e words
_____
_____
_____
_____
_____
The short e sound can be spelled: e, ea, ai, or ie

short i words
_____
_____
_____
The short i sound can be spelled: i

short u words
_____
_____
The short u sound can be spelled: u

Cool Creatures

Circle the **k** sound in each animal name.

SPELLING AND VOCABULARY

K sounds

An **octopus** has three hearts.

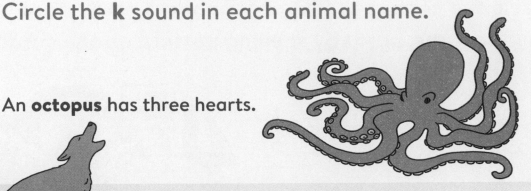

A **coyote** can howl, bark, and yip.

Chickens can fly.

A **caterpillar** has twelve eyes.

Crabs can walk in all directions.

BRAIN BOX

The **k** sound can be spelled with a **k**, **c**, **ch**, or **ck**. For example: **k**ing, **c**oo**k**, s**ch**ool, bri**ck**

A **hawk's** curved, sharp talons help it catch prey.

All but one species of **chipmunk** are found in North America.

Challenge Yourself!

A mollusk is an invertebrate, which means it's an animal without a backbone, usually enclosed by a shell. A clam is an example of a mollusk. Can you circle the **k** sounds in **clam** and in **mollusk**?

Did You Hear That?

Circle the **silent consonant** in each word.

Some words have more than one.

night · write · autumn · campaign · comb · raspberry · wrong · gnome · climb · knowledge · right · doubt

Write a sentence using a **silent b** word.

_____

Write a sentence using a **silent k** word.

_____

Write a sentence using a **silent gh** word.

_____

Write a sentence using a **silent p** word.

_____

BRAIN BOX

Silent **consonants** are letters that become silent when combined with other letters. For example:

w as in wrist
k as in knock
b as in thumb
gh as in eight
g as in sign
p as in cupboard
h as in why
n as in column
d as in ledge

Double or Nothing

Rewrite each word using **-ing**.

SPELLING AND VOCABULARY

Words ending in **-ed** or **-ing**

swim <u>swimming</u>

write _____

dream _____

run _____

jump _____

dig _____

ask _____

change _____

drive _____

win _____

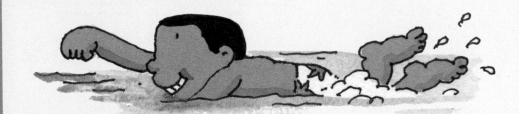

BRAIN BOX

Follow these rules when adding **-ed** or **-ing** to a word:

• If a word ends in a **silent e**, drop the **e**:

hope = hop**ed**, hop**ing**

• If a word ends in a single vowel followed by a single consonant, double the consonant:

hop = hop**ped**, hop**ping**

• If a word ends in a consonant followed by the letter **y**, add **-ing** or change the **y** to **i** before adding **-ed**:

carry = carry**ing**, carr**ied**

Write one sentence that uses at least two of the **-ing** words above.

_____
_____
_____
_____

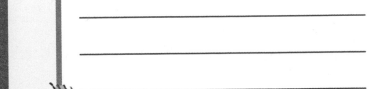

Rewrite each word using **-ed**.

wish _____   nod _____

shop _____   laugh _____

live _____   smile _____

shine _____   scrub _____

hurry _____   rely _____

Complete each sentence with a word from the boxes. Change the spelling and be sure to add **-ed** or **-ing**.

worry	rob
pop	sneeze
slip	wave

I am _____ about my social studies test tomorrow.

I started _____ when I smelled the flowers.

The father _____ to his daughters as they got on the bus.

Everyone jumped when he _____ the balloons.

He started _____ on the icy driveway.

The thief _____ the bank.

14

Orderly Neighbors

Complete each word with **ie** or **ei**.

You see your w _e_ _i_ ght when you get on a scale.

Another word for "get" is "rec __ __ ve."

A person who steals something is a th __ __ f.

Santa rides a sl __ __ gh on Christmas Eve.

We did an experiment in sc __ __ nce.

The number after seven is __ __ ght.

The puzzle is missing one p __ __ ce.

If I ever saw a ghost, I would shr __ __ k!

A fr __ __ ght train carries heavy loads.

A ch __ __ f is the leader of a tribe.

BRAIN BOX

When **i** and **e** are side-by-side, the **i** usually comes before the **e**, except after **c**. For example: grief, friend, receive, deceit

When **i** and **e** make a **long a** sound, **e** comes before the **i**. For example: neighbor, vein

Circle the **ie** and **ei** words in the word search below. Words go across or down.

D	B	K	G	A	S	C	I	E	N	C	E	F	U
M	Y	R	U	O	Z	L	J	D	R	B	H	R	S
S	W	E	I	G	H	T	X	D	C	H	I	E	F
V	B	C	M	V	S	H	R	I	E	K	V	I	F
P	I	E	C	E	N	I	C	A	L	A	J	G	L
O	C	I	G	S	L	E	I	G	H	O	S	H	R
H	D	V	K	Q	U	F	T	B	I	X	H	T	T
X	A	E	I	G	H	T	B	O	F	B	R	C	K

Right and Wrong

Circle each misspelled word in the boxes.

(Febuary)	enuf	shoping	favrit
busy	because	once	hitting
dinasor	suprise	Wensday	receive
peeple	anser	minit	docter
please	calendar	kwite	giving

SPELLING AND VOCABULARY

Commonly misspelled words

Write the correct spelling of each misspelled word on the lines below.

D...I...N...O...

February _____ _____

_____ _____ _____

_____ _____ _____

_____ _____ _____

Write a joke using two or more words you spelled correctly.

_____

_____

Write a sentence using two of the words you spelled correctly.

_____

_____

The More the Merrier

Write the **plural** for each word.

knife _knives_   calf _____

city _____   glass _____

shelf _____   brush _____

penny _____   tax _____

witch _____   candy _____

turkey _____ ray _____

SPELLING AND VOCABULARY

Plurals

BRAIN BOX

There are special rules for changing some words from singular to **plural**:

• If a noun ends in **sh, ch, ss,** or **x,** add **es.** For example: box ⟶ boxes

• If a noun ends in a consonant followed by a **y,** change the **y** to **i** and add **es.** For example: berry ⟶ berries

• If a noun ends in a vowel followed by a **y,** add **s.** For example: toy ⟶ toys

For many nouns ending in **f** or **fe,** change the **f** or **fe** to **v** and add **es.** For example: loaf ⟶ loaves

What other words follow these special plural rules? Write the plural form of as many words as you can think of on the cards.

Nouns ending in **sh, ch, ss, x**

Nouns ending in a consonant followed by **y**

Nouns ending in a vowel followed by **y**

Nouns ending in **f** or **fe**

Two's Company

Write the **plural** for each word.

Then circle the plural forms in the word search.
Words go across and down.

Plurals

baby

house

peach

fox

babies

_____

_____

_____

bunny

boy

puppy

elf

_____

_____

_____

_____

spy

_____

tiger

_____

S	P	I	E	S	Y	E	Q	W	J	L	S
X	V	O	G	U	E	I	T	M	U	N	Y
P	U	B	A	B	I	E	S	H	O	Y	X
U	L	O	Q	W	K	N	E	I	B	G	S
P	J	Y	I	C	P	H	L	T	L	P	L
P	W	S	O	B	U	N	N	I	E	S	M
I	U	K	L	C	P	H	Q	G	A	D	F
E	L	V	E	S	U	Z	I	E	V	Z	F
S	D	I	Q	W	B	M	Y	R	E	R	O
M	R	H	O	U	S	E	S	S	S	B	X
C	I	K	F	M	C	K	W	V	L	I	E
B	V	Q	M	H	P	E	A	C	H	E	S

Rule Breakers

Fill in the blanks to write the **irregular plural** for each oddball word.

SPELLING AND VOCABULARY

Irregular plurals

child	child <u>ren</u>	goose	g __ __ se
mouse	m __ __ e	woman	wom __ n
man	m __ n	ox	ox __ __
tooth	t __ __ th	fish	f __ sh
sheep	sh __ __ p	moose	m __ __ se

Finish the story using at least five **irregular plurals**.

The children went to the zoo yesterday. _____

_____

_____

_____

_____

_____

Draw a picture to go with your story.

BRAIN BOX

Some words don't follow the rules for making plurals. These are called **irregular plurals**.

Special Beginnings

Complete each word using a **prefix** below.

| re | pre | mis | sub |

Prefixes

I saw that movie before any of my friends saw it.
I went to a _pre_ view of it the day before it opened.

My dog is well trained, but yesterday he _____ behaved
by jumping up on our best living room chair.

My little sister knocked over her tower of blocks.
Now she has to _____ build it.

The bricks were starting to crumble off the side
of the building. The construction of the building
must be _____ standard.

He got only one word wrong on his spelling test.
He _____ spelled the word "horrible."

The cookbook said to _____ heat the oven
for thirty minutes before putting in the cake.

My dad painted the kitchen purple, but the color
seemed wrong to him. Now he wants
to _____ paint the room.

BRAIN BOX

A **prefix** is a group of letters that changes the meaning of a word when added to the beginning of the word.

For example, the prefix **sub** means *below*. A **sub**zero temperature is a temperature below zero.

The prefix **re** means *again*. To **re**write a word means to write it again.

The prefix **pre** means *before*. **Pre**school is the school a child attends before elementary school.

The prefix **mis** means *badly*, *mistakenly*, or *incorrectly*. Socks that are **mis**matched do not match or are matched incorrectly.

That's a Negative

Complete each word using a **prefix** below.

dis	im	in	un

SPELLING AND
VOCABULARY

Prefixes

I was so _____ happy when we lost the baseball game!

I can hardly wait to _____ wrap my birthday presents.

I am _____ patient to read my book.

It is _____ polite to talk with your mouth full.

The toys are on sale. I can buy two because they are _____ expensive.

My brothers and I sometimes _____ agree about who should sit by the window.

At first, climbing the hill seemed _____ possible, but we stuck with it and got to the top.

Although I _____ like brussels sprouts, I love most vegetables.

I form my own opinions. I am an _____ dependent thinker.

BRAIN BOX

The prefixes **dis-, in-, im-,** and **un-** mean *not* or *the opposite of.* For example, *disinterested* means *not interested.*

Write a sentence using at least two words with prefixes.

_____

_____

What's Back There?

Read each sentence. Find the missing word in one of the boxes and then add **-ful** or **-less** to make it correct.

hope	thought	fear	use
care	color	power	help

Dylan loved the feeling of taking off in an airplane. He could feel how <u>powerful</u> the engines were.

Sharise's aunt is _____ . She sends Sharise a special card every holiday.

Ming is _____ when it comes to gymnastics. He'll try just about anything.

Cole is not the fastest runner in the class, but he is still _____ that he will win the race.

I love helping my mom cook dinner and set the table. It makes me feel like I'm being _____ .

I like trying to spot bright, cheery butterflies. The more _____ , the better!

Arguing with my sister is _____ . She is so stubborn!

He was so _____ with the paint. It splattered all over the floor.

BRAIN BOX

A **suffix** is a group of letters that changes the meaning of a word when added to the ending of a word.

For example, the suffix **-ful** means *full of.* A cheer**ful** person is someone who is full of cheer.

The suffix **-less** means *to be without something.* A cheer**less** person is someone who lacks cheer.

What's My Job?

Label each picture using a word from the boxes.

Add **-er**, **-or**, **-ist**, or **-ian** to complete the word.

Suffixes

violin	write	magic	dance
sing	teach	act	art

teacher   _____   _____

_____   _____   _____

BRAIN BOX

The suffixes -er, -or, -ist, and -ian mean
someone who. For example:

farmer = someone who works on a farm

editor = someone who edits

cellist = someone who plays the cello

comedian = someone who performs comedy

_____   _____

A Cloudy Day

A **prefix** or **suffix** has been added to each of these words. Underline the **root word** (or base word) in each word. Then circle the prefix or suffix.

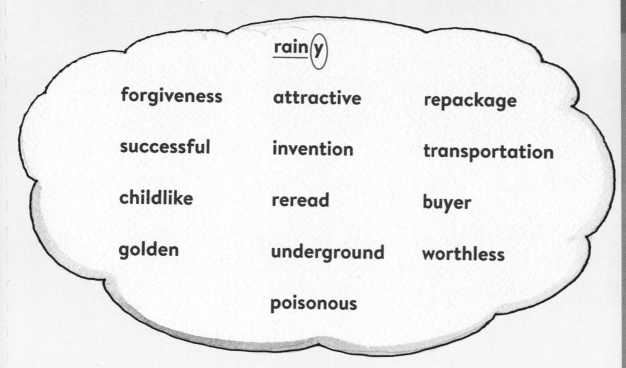

rain(y)

forgiveness   attractive   repackage

successful   invention   transportation

childlike   reread   buyer

golden   underground   worthless

poisonous

Write a sentence using one of these words. Then draw a picture to match your sentence.

_____

_____

BRAIN BOX

The word to which a **prefix** or a **suffix** has been added is called a **root word** (or a base word). For example, in the word *cloudy*, the root word is *cloud*.

All About Antonyms

Circle the word that is the **antonym** of the word in bold.

Antonyms

late	early	tardy
night	dark	day
fast	slow	quick
dry	clean	wet
sharp	dull	prickly
last	final	first
quiet	loud	calm
enter	exit	arrive
together	pair	alone
near	far	close
off	shut	on
full	high	empty

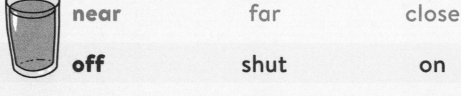

BRAIN BOX

Two words that have the opposite meaning are called **antonyms**. For example, *strong* and *weak* are antonyms.

Bonus!

What is the antonym of **north**?

_____

What is the antonym of **east**?

_____

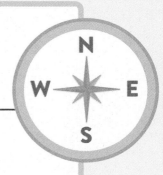

Something in Common

Draw a line to match each pair of **synonyms**.

hungry	construct
angry	excited
elevated	cruel
eager	famished
pal	boast
build	rich
wicked	mad
brag	moist
wealthy	high
damp	friend

Write two other synonyms in the boxes below.
Then draw a picture to show what they mean.

BRAIN BOX

Words that have the same or nearly the same meaning are called **synonyms**. For example, *dish* and *plate* are synonyms.

Two for One

Write a **synonym** and an **antonym** for each word on the chart. Use the words from the boxes below.

ill	break	different	difficult
false	begin	depart	repair
factual	arrive	laugh	energetic
complete	exhausted	alike	cautious
sob	easy	healthy	reckless

	Synonym	**Antonym**
careful	cautious	reckless
cry		
hard		
leave		
tired		
fix		
sick		
finish		
similar		
true		

An Ant on My Aunt!

Complete each sentence with the correct **homophones**.

night   knight

write   right

threw   through

meet   meat

there   their

Homophones

two   to

one   won

fair   fare

Dee <u>threw</u> the ball <u>through</u> the hole in the wall.

Logan and Maria saw _____ friends over _____ by the hot dog stand.

Jamal wanted _____ eat _____ crackers.

I'll _____ you in the _____ section of the market.

The Fantastic Fumblers have _____ only _____ of their baseball games.

Ms. Ramirez asked us to _____ the _____ answers to the math questions.

The brave _____ spent the _____ in the haunted castle.

He had enough bus _____ to get all the way to the county _____ .

BRAIN BOX

Homophones are words that sound the same but have different spellings and meanings. For example, *groan* and *grown* are homophones.

Let's Write Right!

Complete each sentence with the correct **homophone**.

Homophones

The girls waded in the __creek__ .

I heard a scary __creak__ on the stairs.

creak

creek

allowed

aloud

I like to read _____ to my little sister.

Stop! You're not _____ to go in there.

The rose has a beautiful _____ .

Brad _____ his cousin a funny birthday card.

scent

sent

towed

toad

The little _____ hopped onto a stone.

They _____ his car to the garage for repairs.

I tightened the belt around my _____ .

It's important not to _____ paper.

waist

waste

principal

principle

Mr. Avila is the _____ of our school.

Martin Luther King Jr. was a man of _____ .

I am wearing my favorite _____ of socks.

Kim ate a sandwich and a _____ for lunch.

pear

pair

stationary

stationery

Mia wrote her friend a letter on her new _____ .

My dad works out on a _____ bike at the gym.

Be a Word Detective

Use the **context clues** in each sentence to figure out the meaning of the highlighted word. Circle the correct definition.

Mr. Ferris was infuriated when the boys hit a baseball through his living room window.
  a. delighted   (b. very angry)   c. interested

Context clues

The tired farmer had toiled in her field all day planting crops.
  a. played   b. run   c. worked hard

The delicious aroma of the cookies baking in the oven made everyone hungry.
  a. smell   b. color   c. heat

Mr. Garcia ascended the ladder to reach the roof of his house.
  a. climbed up   b. climbed down   c. took away

The expert declared, "This is an authentic coin from ancient Rome, so it's extremely valuable."
  a. dirty   b. common   c. real

The queen's throne was very elaborate; it was covered with gold and jewels.
  a. soft   b. normal   c. fancy

The police officer admonished the man not to drive down the flooded street.
  a. rewarded   b. promised   c. warned

Because we had such a hectic weekend, we barely had a moment to rest.
  a. slow   b. busy   c. annoying

BRAIN BOX

When you come across a word you don't understand, you can often figure out its meaning by looking at the surrounding words. These words are called **context clues.**

What Does That Mean?

Use the **context clues** in each sentence to figure out the meaning of the highlighted word.

Then find the correct definition on the cards and write it on the line.

easily noticed	dangerous	very important

rich	lay back	calm	worn down	amazed

It is (crucial) <u>very important</u> to win the game if we want to be in the state championship playoffs.

Only the bravest climbers attempted to climb the (hazardous) _____ mountain.

I was (flabbergasted) _____ when he told me he was really a space alien.

The inventor was so (prosperous) _____ that they lived in a mansion and had their own private airplane.

The tired boy (reclined) _____ on the sofa and soon fell asleep.

The boat sailed smoothly on the (tranquil) _____ lake.

The building was so (dilapidated) _____ that it was falling apart.

The (conspicuous) _____ man wore a red wig and a bright purple suit.

Put 'Em In Order

Number each group of words to show the correct **alphabetical order**.

__2__ race

__1__ rabbit

__3__ rose

_____ messy

_____ meat

_____ more

_____ map

_____ mouse

_____ mad

_____ has

_____ home

_____ hill

_____ ride

_____ red

_____ read

_____ heavy

_____ happy

_____ hide

_____ hall

_____ hero

_____ hello

_____ rest

_____ road

_____ rug

_____ money

_____ mitten

_____ minus

BRAIN BOX

When putting words in **alphabetical order**, sort using the first letter of each word. For example: *apple, banana, cantaloupe*

If the first letter of two or more words is the same, sort using the second letter. For example: with *best* and *bat*, **bat** comes before **best**.

If the first and second letter is the same, use the third letter to determine alphabetical order. For example: with *dance* and *date*, **dance** comes before **date**.

Look It Up

Read about how to use a **dictionary**.

A **dictionary** can tell you what a word means and how to spell and pronounce it. The words in a dictionary are listed in **alphabetical order**. Every word listed in a dictionary is called an **entry word**.

For every entry word, you'll usually find:
- the word broken down by syllable
- a pronunciation guide
- an abbreviation for the part of speech
- one or more definitions (if there is more than one meaning, the definitions will be numbered)

PRONUNCIATION GUIDE

ENTRY WORD

PART OF SPEECH

DEFINITION

con • cen • trate (kan sen trāt), *v.* **1.** to bring together in one place **2.** to make thicker or stronger **3.** to pay attention

Pronunciation Key

a short a	**i** short i	**u** short u
ā long a	**ī** long i	**ū** long u as in mule
e short e	**o** short o	**u̇** long u as in brook
ē long e	**ō** long o	**ü** long u as is fool

Abbreviation Key

n = noun   v = verb   adj = adjective

adv = adverb   pron = pronoun

BRAIN BOX

You can use a **print** or **online dictionary** to look up words. Words in print dictionaries are listed one right after another in alphabetical order, page after page. At the top of each page in a print dictionary are two **guide words**. The word on the left is the first entry word on the page. The word on the right is the last entry word on the page. To look up a word in an online dictionary, type the word in the search bar.

Use this dictionary page to answer the questions.

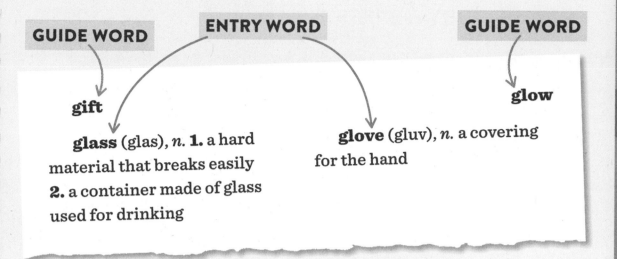

GUIDE WORD   **ENTRY WORD**   **GUIDE WORD**

gift   **glow**

glass (glas), *n.* **1.** a hard material that breaks easily **2.** a container made of glass used for drinking

glove (gluv), *n.* a covering for the hand

What are the two guide words on the sample dictionary page?

_____

What is the last word included on this page?

_____

Would the word *globe* be included on the page?

_____

Ask an adult before you go online.

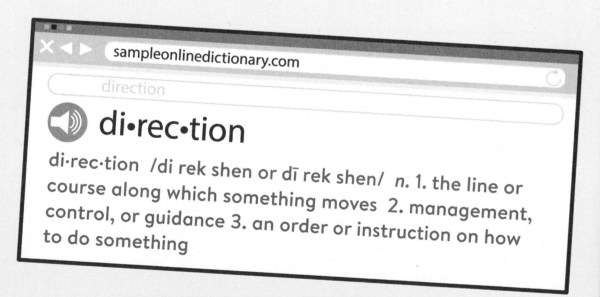

sampleonlinedictionary.com

direction

di•rec•tion

di•rec•tion /di rek shen or dī rek shen/ *n.* **1.** the line or course along which something moves **2.** management, control, or guidance **3.** an order or instruction on how to do something

What part of speech is the entry word?

_____

How many syllables are in the entry word? _____

Word Search

Look up each word in the dictionary.

Write the definition in the box. Then use the word in a sentence.

Dictionary skills

chemical

_____

_____

_____

_____

electricity

_____

_____

_____

_____

wonder

_____

_____

_____

_____

LANGUAGE ARTS

Do you think it's a piece of cake to list words that rhyme with *blue*? If so, you'll love this next section! Let's try to *throw you for a loop* or see if you're as *sharp as a knife.*

PARENTS In this section, your child will have fun with words while learning about analogies, similes, and idioms. If your child is an English learner, take time to make sure they understand the content and mechanics as they "play" with words and sentences.

For additional resources, visit www.BrainQuest.com/grade3

Compound words

Getting Together

Draw a line from each word in column A to a word in column B to make a **common compound** word. Then write the compound words in column C.

A	**B**	**C**
straw	tail	strawberry
eye	walk	
wheel	brow	
side	ground	
pony	fly	
pepper	berry	
butter	mint	
play	barrow	

Now find the **compound words** in the word search.

BRAIN BOX

A **compound word** is formed when two words are joined together. For example: sun + flower = sunflower.

H	W	K	J	W	P	O	N	Y	T	A	I	L	F	A
A	H	B	G	B	L	V	I	P	F	C	E	L	B	Q
B	E	S	T	R	A	W	B	E	R	R	Y	P	D	E
U	E	D	L	T	Y	L	M	P	J	M	E	D	I	O
T	L	F	A	H	G	E	H	P	L	C	B	E	R	A
T	B	I	B	F	R	A	C	E	B	G	R	B	G	P
E	A	N	B	U	O	D	K	R	F	E	O	N	J	V
R	R	J	P	D	U	V	J	M	P	O	W	G	U	N
F	R	G	A	K	N	K	S	I	D	E	W	A	L	K
L	O	Q	M	S	D	O	Q	N	H	S	I	V	S	R
Y	W	K	C	H	K	M	D	T	H	T	Y	B	T	F
F	A	D	L	Q	R	K	J	O	B	B	L	A	I	C

Circle the **compound words** in the sentences.

He tiptoed down the (hallway) to his (bedroom).

Campbell's dad always wears a necktie to work.

Everyone was going to the big basketball game on Friday night.

She was afraid of being stung by a jellyfish.

There's nothing better than a cozy turtleneck in the wintertime.

Taryn likes to look for starfish on the beach.

They needed to buy a fishbowl for the goldfish.

Ericka and her friends knew the record snowfall meant they could build the biggest snowman ever.

Compound words

Choose three compound words from above. Write each part of the compound word in the spaces below. Then write the whole word.

Word 1		Word 2		Compound word
	+		=	
	+		=	
	+		=	

Word Scramble

Unscramble the following words. Then rearrange the boxed letters to find the fifth word.

Scrambled
words

Colors

c l a b k _ _ ☐ _ _

e g n e r ☐ _ _ _ ☐

r e p p u l _ _ ☐ _ _ ☐

w e l y o l _ _ _ _ ☐ _

☐ ☐ ☐ ☐ ☐ ☐

Mammals

y e m k o n _ ☐ _ ☐ _ _

r o h i n _ _ _ ☐ ☐

d a n a p _ ☐ _ _ ☐

g r o a l l i ☐ _ ☐ _ _ _ _

☐ ☐ ☐ ☐ ☐ ☐ ☐ ☐

The Human Body

n i r a b _ _ _ _ ☐

l n u g s _ _ _ _ ☐

r a t h e _ ☐ _ _ _

d o b l o ☐ _ ☐ _ _

☐ ☐ ☐ ☐ ☐

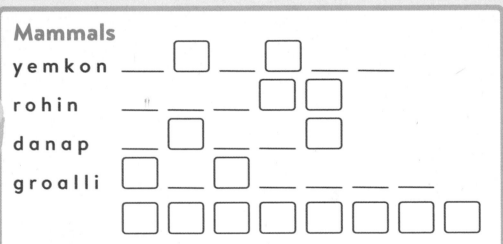

Rhyme Time

Circle the word that does not rhyme with the word in the box.

| her | were | (where) | stir | fur |

| scratch | catch | hatch | watch | match |

| ball | fall | stall | small | shall |

| head | bead | fed | said | dead |

| purred | word | heard | beard | bird |

| care | fare | bare | are | dare |

| stone | phone | moan | gone | bone |

| wood | could | stood | mood | hood |

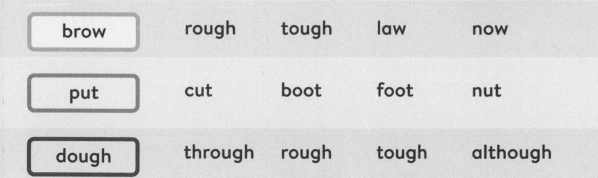

Circle the word that rhymes with the word in the box.

| brow | rough | tough | law | now |

| put | cut | boot | foot | nut |

| dough | through | rough | tough | although |

Clapping and Tapping

Count the **syllables** in each word below.

Then sort the words on the cards.

Syllables

spelling	question	operator	ladder
biography	dinosaur	birthday	adorable
bumblebee	caterpillar	accident	grandmother

two-syllable words

spelling

_____

_____

_____

three-syllable words

_____

_____

_____

four-syllable words

_____

_____

_____

Presto Change-o!

Start with the first word in the list. Change just one letter to create a new word that fits the next clue.

Continue down the list, changing one letter from the previous word to fit each clue.

it might make you invisible	c l o a k
the sound a frog makes	c r o a k
a dishonest person	_ _ _ _ _
a small body of water	_ _ _ _ _
something a witch rides	_ _ _ _ _

Word play

a hair color	b l o n d
it flows through your veins	_ _ _ _ _
to overflow with water	_ _ _ _ _
it's opposite the ceiling	_ _ _ _ _
an ingredient in a cake	_ _ _ _ _

Now write your own word play puzzle.
Then give it to a friend to solve.

_____   _____
_____   _____
_____   _____
_____   _____
_____   _____

It's All Relative

Complete each **analogy** using a word below.

water	green	girl	food
pounds	patient	day	string

Analogies

Piano is to *key* as *guitar* is to _____.

Sky is to *blue* as *grass* is to _____.

Moon is to *night* as *sun* is to _____.

Teacher is to *student* as *doctor* is to _____.

Brother is to *boy* as *sister* is to _____.

Height is to *inches* as *weight* is to _____.

Thirsty is to *water* as *hungry* is to _____.

Car is to *road* as *boat* is to _____.

BRAIN BOX

An **analogy** compares how things are related to each other.

For example: *Hat* is to *head* as *shoe* is to *foot*. A hat is **worn** on a head just like a shoe is **worn** on a foot.

Use your imagination to finish
the analogies.

Roar is to *lion* as _____ .

Scale is to *fish* as _____ .

January is to *winter* as _____ .

Analogies

Yesterday is to *past* as _____ .

Hammer is to *pound* as _____ .

Now draw a picture of your favorite analogy.

Construction Zone

Write the two words that make up each **contraction**.

Contractions

couldn't

could

not

she's

_____

_____

didn't

_____

_____

they're

_____

_____

what's

_____

_____

weren't

_____

_____

don't

_____

_____

we'll

_____

_____

he'd

_____

_____

it's

_____

_____

BRAIN BOX

A **contraction** is two words joined together. When the two words are joined, some of the letters in the second word are replaced by an apostrophe. For example: The contraction for *have not* is *haven't*.

It's Me, Connor!

Replace the highlighted words with a **contraction** from the boxes below.

he's	couldn't	we've
I've	I'm	what's
I'll	weren't	they're

Dear Aunt Shelly,

(I am) ＿＿＿＿＿＿ writing this letter to you from Camp Walnut Creek. I love camp so far! (I have) ＿＿＿＿＿＿ already made a lot of cool friends. My bunkmate is named Ben, and (he is) ＿＿＿＿＿＿ a really good soccer player. (We have) ＿＿＿＿＿＿ been kicking the ball around every day. My two other friends are Thomas and Oliver. (They are) ＿＿＿＿＿＿ identical twins! If it (were not) ＿＿＿＿＿＿ for the different way they dress, I (could not) ＿＿＿＿＿＿ tell them apart! I have to go now, so (I will) ＿＿＿＿＿＿ say goodbye. Please write back and tell me (what is) ＿＿＿＿＿＿ happening back home!

Love,
Connor

Now pretend you're Aunt Shelly and write a short letter back to Connor. Use three contractions.

＿＿＿＿＿＿＿＿＿＿＿＿＿＿＿＿＿＿＿＿＿＿

＿＿＿＿＿＿＿＿＿＿＿＿＿＿＿＿＿＿＿＿＿＿

＿＿＿＿＿＿＿＿＿＿＿＿＿＿＿＿＿＿＿＿＿＿

＿＿＿＿＿＿＿＿＿＿＿＿＿＿＿＿＿＿＿＿＿＿

A Figure of Speech

Complete each **simile** with a clue from the next page.

The baby frog was as light as a <u>feather</u> .

I'm so thirsty, my mouth is as dry as a _____.

Similes

Even under pressure, Shanti is as cool as _____.

The boy tiptoed down the hallway, quiet as a _____.

The center on the basketball team was as tall as a _____.

He turned as white as a _____ when he saw how high the roller coaster was.

If my kitten keeps eating so much, she will become as big as an _____.

BRAIN BOX

A **simile** is a phrase or figure of speech that compares two things using the words *as* or *like*. For example: The dancer was *as graceful as a swan*. This phrase compares a dancer with a swan.

Now make up a simile and draw your own clue on the blank card.

_____

_____

Similes

desert

skyscraper

feather

mouse

ice

ghost

elephant

Whatever Do You Mean?

Write what you think each highlighted idiom really means.

Lori spilled the beans . Now everyone knows my secret.

_____

_____

Ronald loves to go to the library. He always has his nose in a book .

_____

_____

Can you give me a hand ? I can't lift the box.

_____

_____

I can't wait to hear about the party. I'm all ears .

_____

_____

That story about the howling ghost made my hair stand on end .

_____

_____

BRAIN BOX

Idioms are expressions that mean something different from what the words might seem to actually say. For example: *hold your tongue* is an idiom that means *be quiet.*

I knew every answer on the science test. It was a piece of cake.

_____

_____

Is your dad really an astronaut, or are you pulling my leg ?

_____

_____

Max and Sybil both like to skate and play chess. They're like two peas in a pod .

_____

_____

The sound of fingernails on a chalkboard drives me up a wall .

_____

_____

Choose an idiom and draw a silly picture of what the words **literally** seem to say.

People, Places, and Things

Read the story.

Underline all the nouns that name a **person** in blue.

Underline all the nouns that name a **place** in green.

Underline all the nouns that name a **thing** in red.

Nouns

A Trip to the Wetland

by Elissa

   Today, our class took a trip to a local wetland with our teacher, Ms. Casamo. The tour guide, Ranger Sala, walked us around. In a wetland, she said, water covers the land, and plants grow in wet soil. Here, many animals such as frogs, salamanders, snakes, and birds make their home. Ranger Sala asked if anyone could name a wetland. Antonio asked whether Everglades National Park, in Florida, is a wetland.

   "It is!" Sala said. "And did you know that it is the only spot on Earth where both alligators and crocodiles live together?"

   Before we left, I saw a bird called a great blue heron standing in the water. It was so still, I thought it might be a statue!

BRAIN BOX

A **noun** is a word that names a person, place, or thing.

Generally Speaking

Circle the **proper nouns** and underline the **common nouns** in the sentences. Then sort each noun on the cards below.

(Ms. Ramos) took our <u>class</u> to the <u>zoo</u>.

MAPLE ST.

In January, Penny moved into her new house on Maple Street.

Common and proper nouns

The Grand Canyon is in Arizona.

SUGAR SHACK

Dylan tied the shoelaces on his shoes.

Aunt Ethel bought delicious doughnuts at the Sugar Shack.

Dr. Pollock took his family to the beach on Sunday.

CLOSED ON LABOR DAY

The pool is closed on Labor Day.

Proper Nouns

Ms. Ramos _____

_____ _____

_____ _____

_____ _____

_____ _____

Common Nouns

class   zoo

_____ _____

_____ _____

_____ _____

_____ _____

BRAIN BOX

A **common noun** names **any** person, place, or thing. Common nouns begin with a lowercase letter. For example: girl, state, day

A **proper noun** is the name of a **specific** person, place, or thing. Proper nouns begin with a capital letter. For example: Wendy, Indiana, Monday

Introducing Nouns

Circle the correct **article** before each word.

 a an apple

 the a magazines

 a an umbrella

 the a shoes

 the an glove

 a an fish

 an the candle

 a an pineapple

 the an oranges

 a an energy bar

 the a balloons

 the an plant

BRAIN BOX

An **article** is a word that goes before a noun. A, *an*, and *the* are all articles.

When the noun begins with a consonant, use *a* or *the*.

When the noun begins with a vowel, use *an* or *the*.

In most cases, if the noun is plural, use *the*.

You, Me, and Them

Circle the correct **pronoun** for the sentences below. Some pronouns are singular, some are plural, and some can be either singular or plural.

List of Pronouns

SINGULAR	I You He She It They	Me You Him Her It Them	My Your His Her Its Their	Mine Yours His Hers Its Theirs
PLURAL	We You They	Us You Them	Our Your Their	Ours Yours Theirs

The dinosaur skeleton was so tall (**it**, their) hit the ceiling.

Nana said (she, her) would take (me, mine) to school today.

Plants need light, water, and nutrient-rich soil so (they, it) can grow.

Lucas said (him, he) was practicing for the spelling bee every day.

Everyone should bring (their, them) pencils to class tomorrow.

Cora and I were so excited to see the parade, (us, we) arrived an hour early.

I didn't see who returned the book to (my, me). (They, Them) left it on (me, my) desk before school.

Squirrels bury nuts so (they, it) can eat in the winter.

The teacher said students should contact (they, them) with any questions.

The class that raised the most money for the animal shelter was (we, ours)!

BRAIN BOX

Pronouns are words that are used in place of nouns. For example:

Ed is wearing a new hat.

He is wearing a new hat. (*He* takes the place of *Ed*.)

A **singular pronoun** takes the place of a singular noun.

A **plural pronoun** takes the place of a plural noun. *They* can take the place of a singular or plural noun.

Whose Is It?

Complete each sentence with the correct
possessive pronoun from the boxes below.

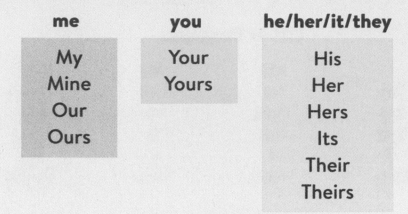

me	you	he/her/it/they
My	Your	His
Mine	Yours	Her
Our		Hers
Ours		Its
		Their
		Theirs

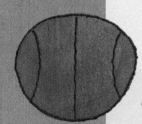

"Whose basketball is this?" asked Elle.
"It belongs to Jon," said Yuri.
"It is __his/theirs__.
His dad got it for __his/their__ birthday."

"Whose bike is this?" asked Morgan.
"It belongs to me," said Betsy. "It's _____.
Look, it has _____ initials on the seat."

BRAIN BOX

A possessive pronoun
shows ownership. For
example: Teri owns
a camera. It is **hers.**
Her camera is new.

"Whose dog is this?" asked Tamika.
"It belongs to us," said the twins.
"It is _____.
_____ dog's name
is Buster."

"Whose sweatshirt is this?" Brian asked Claire.
"I saw you wear it yesterday, and it's _____
favorite color. I think it must be _____."

"Whose ice skates are these?" asked Milo.
"They belong to Liz," said Mrs. Randall.
"I know they are _____
because _____ skates
have blue laces."

"Whose books are these?" asked Madison.
"They belong to those boys," said Suzie.
"I'm sure they are _____ .
They always leave _____
 books lying around."

"Whose parrot is this?" asked Eduardo.
"It belongs to me," said Katie.
"I should put it back in _____ cage."

Noun Ownership

Rewrite these wordy sentences by changing the highlighted words to **possessive nouns**. You may have to switch around some of the other words in the sentence.

The reading contest of my teacher is going to start next week.

<u>My teacher's reading contest is</u>
<u>going to start next week.</u>

I didn't realize that was the house belonging to Sari .

_____

_____

The cupcakes of Samantha were absolutely delicious!

_____

_____

That Halloween party of my friend was a little spooky.

_____

_____

Did you know that this trumpet belongs to Lalo ?

_____

I promised I would clean out the car of my dad .

_____

The sister of Kody won the spelling bee.

_____

BRAIN BOX

When nouns are **possessive**, they tell who or what owns something else. Singular nouns are made possessive by adding an apostrophe and an **s**.

For example:
The dog that belongs to Jeff can also be written as *Jeff's dog.*

The **possessive nouns** in these sentences are missing their **apostrophes**. Fill in the apostrophes so the sentences make sense.

All of my friends' costumes look great!

I love to hear my English teachers stories.

That trees leaves are starting to turn color.

Mollys birthday is the day after tomorrow.

That girls outfit looks just like mine.

Jamie couldn't believe how high the giraffes necks reached.

Choose a noun below to complete each sentence. Then change the noun to a plural possessive and write it on the line.

| teacher | girl |
| traveler | bull |

The <u>teachers'</u> lounge is on the second floor.

The _____ horns are white and gray.

The _____ rest stop has the best doughnuts in town.

The team gathered in the _____ locker room.

BRAIN BOX

To make a **plural noun** ending in s possessive, put the apostrophe after the s. For example:

The dogs' dish (two or more dogs have one dish)

The dogs' dishes (two or more dogs have two or more dishes)

It's All in the Details

Underline the **adjectives** in the following descriptions. Then sort them on the cards below.

Adjectives

<u>three</u> <u>enormous</u> and <u>sweet-smelling</u> sunflowers

two delicious, meatless pizzas

five spicy roasted peppers

a tiny, brown, loud bird

a large, blue pool

the noisy timpani drums

the quiet gray kitten

Taste or Smell

<u>sweet-smelling</u>

_____

_____

Color

_____

_____

_____

Number

<u>three</u>

_____

_____

Size

<u>enormous</u>

_____

_____

Kind

_____

_____

_____

Sound

_____

_____

_____

BRAIN BOX

Adjectives are words that describe nouns. Adjectives can tell how many or what size, shape, color, or kind. They can tell how something feels, looks, tastes, sounds, or smells. Adjectives make writing more interesting.

Slimy Snails and Wiggly Worms

Write a creative **adjective** in front of each noun.

For a challenge, try to find an adjective that starts with the same sound as the noun.

Adjectives

<u>dreadful</u> dinosaur

<u>marvelous</u> movie

_____ shirt

_____ dinner

_____ wizard

_____ friend

_____ dog

_____ cat

_____ bug

_____ elf

More or Most?

Write the correct form of the highlighted adjective in each sentence.

Adjectives that compare

This paper feels (rough) _rougher_ than the other one.

He is always the (hungry) _____ of all the boys.

She is the (fast) _____ runner in the school.

A zebra is (short) _____ than a giraffe.

My turtle was the (slow) _____ in the race.

That's the (bright) _____ color I've ever seen.

Circle the incorrect adjective in each sentence. Then write the correct adjective in the box.

BRAIN BOX

When comparing two nouns, add **-er** to adjectives to mean "more." For example: This bird is **louder** means that one bird is more loud than the other bird.

When comparing more than two nouns, add **-est** to adjectives to mean "most." For example: This bird is the **loudest** on our street means that this bird is the most loud.

If the adjective ends in a consonant followed by a **y**, turn the **y** into an **i** before adding **-est**. For example: Will was the **happiest** boy on the team.

When comparing adjectives that are three or more syllables, use "more" or "most" before the adjective. For example: Green is a more popular color than purple. Green is the most popular color in third grade. Populerer and populerest don't sound right!

Some adjectives that compare are irregular. For example:

• good, better, best

• bad, worse, worst

• far, farther, farthest

I think ham tastes much gooder than chicken.

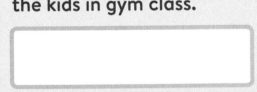

Seth ran the farest of all the kids in gym class.

Jan's room is cluttered, but Todd's is even badder!

Seize the Day!

Circle the correct form of the **verb** in each sentence.

Hannah bowl (bowls) every Saturday with her dad.

Seth and Arturo always figure figures out the answer before anyone else.

The fan work works really well when you put it on full power.

My cats investigate investigates every little spider and ant they see on the ground.

Each Halloween, Sydney dress dresses in a different costume.

Sophie prepare prepares for her game by doing drills in the backyard.

Don't you think we dance dances well together?

Jamal and his sister read reads several books every week.

BRAIN BOX

A **present-tense verb** tells about something that is happening now. For example: Colin **plays** soccer.

If a verb describes the action of one person or thing, it usually ends in s or -es. For example: The swan **floats** on the pond.

If a verb describes the action of more than one person or thing, the verb usually remains as it is, without adding s or -es. For example: The swans **float** on the pond.

Past, Present, Future

Underline the **verb** in each sentence. Then write **past**, **present**, or **future** to tell when the action is happening.

The twins <u>will</u> <u>go</u> to camp next summer. | future |

Javi's pet lizard eats crickets. | |

Our dad cooked steak on the grill last night. | |

My uncle always sings in the shower. | |

Serena hunted everywhere for her missing cat. | |

I lived in Michigan when I was a baby. | |

José walks to school with his best friend. | |

Chloe will ride her bike to the store. | |

We will plant our garden in the spring. | |

BRAIN BOX

A **past-tense verb** tells about something that has already happened. To change a verb to past tense, add a **d** to most words that end in **e**, and add **-ed** to most other words. For example: Colin **exercised** in the gym last night. Colin **pulled** the rope.

A **future-tense verb** tells about something that will happen in the future. The word **will** is usually used with future tense verbs. For example: Colin **will exercise** outside next weekend.

Write three sentences about what you did last weekend. Then circle all the **past-tense** verbs.

_____

_____

_____

_____

Verbs

Look around the room. Write three sentences about everything that's happening now. Circle all the **present-tense** verbs.

_____

_____

_____

_____

Write three sentences about your plans for next summer's vacation. Circle all the **future-tense** verbs.

_____

_____

_____

_____

_____

Play Ball!

Circle each **action verb** in the story.

Today the Queen Bees (play) the Hornets. In the first inning, Ava hits the ball into left field. Natalie pitches the ball to the next batter.

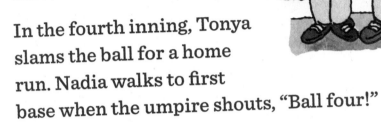

In the fourth inning, Tonya slams the ball for a home run. Nadia walks to first base when the umpire shouts, "Ball four!"

In the eighth inning, Aiko hurts her ankle when she slides into third base. Coach Monroe examines her ankle and then tapes it.

In the last inning, Carmen catches a fly ball to center field for the third out. The Queen Bees win the game by one run!

BRAIN BOX

An **action verb** tells what the subject of a sentence is doing. For example: Ethan **runs** down the court and **passes** the ball to Jamie.

Runs and *passes* are both action verbs because they describe what Ethan is doing.

Match each one with a scrambled action verb below and rewrite it correctly on the line.

malss _____

issled _____

klaws _____

mxienesa _____

ihst _____

shotsu _____

iwn _____

stipche _____

lyap play _____

scathec _____

truhs _____

steap _____

Help Wanted!

Complete each sentence with a **helping verb** from the boxes below.

is	have	has	will	had	are
would	was	were	can	could	am

Helping verbs

The girls _____ standing at the bus stop yesterday.

I _____ searching for my pen last night.

We _____ watching the sky for lightning.

My sister _____ wearing her new jeans today.

We _____ skated on this pond before.

I _____ going to the mall in a few minutes.

Your brother _____ like some more popcorn.

Mrs. Takito _____ baked those cookies before.

By the end of the meet, Jabari _____ win three races.

Now write three of your own sentences using the rest of the helping verbs in the boxes above.

_____

_____

_____

_____

_____

BRAIN BOX

Helping verbs are used before action verbs and can help tell when the action takes place. The movie stars *will* sign autographs. (In this example, **will** is the helping verb letting the reader know the action is in the future.)

Link 'Em Up

Complete each sentence with the correct **linking verb** from the boxes below.

looks	are	is	seems
was	am	feels	smells

Linking verbs

My favorite food _____ hamburgers.

Yesterday I _____ at the pool all day.

I _____ very excited today.

The dogs _____ barking loudly now.

My hamster's fur _____ soft.

This test _____ like it might be hard.

Your hair _____ pretty.

Something _____ bad.

BRAIN BOX

Linking verbs connect a noun to a word or words that tell something about the noun.

For example: Russell **is** happy about the chess tournament.

The linking verb *is* connects Russell to his feelings about the chess tournament.

The Time Machine

Complete each clue by changing the highlighted present-tense verb to an **irregular past-tense** verb. Then complete the crossword puzzle.

Irregular verbs

BRAIN BOX

An **irregular past-tense** verb is a verb in which we don't add -**ed** or **d** to form its past tense, as we do with a regular verb. Some irregular past-tense verbs include **think/thought, break/broke,** and **feel/felt.**

Across

3. Tony (read) _____ his book after dinner.
4. I (give) _____ Adam a computer game for his birthday.
5. Donald (throw) _____ the ball.
7. Janie (ring) _____ the bell after school.
9. He (bring) _____ his violin to school.

Down

1. We (drink) _____ strawberry milkshakes at the diner.
2. Alisha (catch) _____ the ball.
6. Ellie (write) _____ a letter to her friend in Texas.
8. Becky (buy) _____ a new dress at the mall.
10. The frightened cat (hide) _____ under the bed.

Story Time

Circle the **present-tense verbs** in the story. Then rewrite the highlighted sentences in the **past tense**. When you're done, circle all the **irregular verbs**.

Irregular verbs

Today I am going to soccer camp. We will drive four hours to get there. When I get there, I will catch up with my camp friends before dinner.

My camp routine is perfect. I eat breakfast in the mess hall and then spend the morning practicing drills. Then I eat lunch and go to an activity like art, music, or chorus. I always choose chorus and sing my heart out every afternoon. After activities we spend more time playing soccer.

On the last night of camp, we all play a joke on our coaches and wear our pajamas to the game. When it is time to say goodbye, we give each other hugs and promise to stay in touch.

Yesterday I (went) to soccer camp.

How, When, or Where

Underline the **verb** in each sentence. Circle the **adverb**. Then sort the adverbs on the cards below.

Shai <u>plays</u> soccer (outside.)

Samuel played the computer game skillfully.

Did it rain today?

There are mosquitoes everywhere.

The ballerina danced gracefully.

Adverbs

The boys waited patiently for their turn.

Kiko walked upstairs.

The rock star played his guitar yesterday.

Tomorrow, I will eat a burrito for lunch.

how	**when**	**where**
		outside

BRAIN BOX

An adverb is a word that describes a verb. Adverbs tell how, when, or where an action happens. For example: The baby cried loudly. The adverb *loudly* tells how the baby cried.

Many adverbs end with the suffix **-ly.**

Meet in the Middle

In each sentence, draw one line under the subject and two lines under the **predicate**.

Then circle all the **nouns**.

The funny (clown) rode on a tiny (bike.)

The sandy beach was very crowded.

The mothers took their children to the park.

All the dogs began to bark.

The Peterson family is going to the mountains tomorrow.

The grumpy man yelled at the noisy boys.

Christian likes to visit his grandparents.

Dawn won a ribbon at the horse show.

BRAIN BOX

A sentence has two parts, a **subject** and a **predicate**.

The subject tells who or what the sentence is about.

The predicate tells what the subject is or does.
The predicate often begins with the verb.

For example:

The shiny jet	took off from the airport.
subject	predicate

What's the Story?

Choose an **article**, an **adjective**, and a **noun** from the Word Boxes and create a **subject** for each sentence.

Subjects

Articles

a	those
an	our
the	my

Adjectives

shy	sweet
silly	funny
old	crazy

Nouns

owl	kangaroos
seal	comedian
rabbits	grandmother

Article	Adjective	Noun	
A	silly	seal	balanced a ball on its nose.
			built a nest in the tall tree.
			told a very hilarious joke!
			ran away when they saw us.
			couldn't wait to see us.
			knit me a warm sweater.

Picture This

Look at each picture. Complete each sentence with a **predicate**.

The space aliens <u>want to travel to Earth</u>.

I always _____
_____.

Sometimes he _____
_____.

The panda bear _____
_____.

That roller coaster _____
_____.

The audience _____
_____.

The sun _____
_____.

It's in Its Den

Circle the correct word in each sentence.

It's and its

My horse won it's   its first race today.

I hope it's   its ready. I'm really hungry!

You should buy that sweater. It's   Its color is perfect for you.

The elephant and it's   its new baby can now be seen at the zoo.

It's   Its time to leave for the movies.

That's a cute puppy. What is it's   its name?

I wonder if it's   its hot outside today.

Hurry up! It's   Its going to rain soon.

What a pretty bird. It's   Its feathers are a beautiful color.

Have you seen my book? It's   Its not in it's   its usual place on my desk.

Write two sentences about your favorite toy.
Use **it's** in one sentence and **its** in the other.

_____

_____

_____

_____

BRAIN BOX

It's and *its* have different meanings.

Its is a possessive pronoun. For example: The lion licked **its** paw.

It's is a contraction that means *it is*. For example: It's my turn to pitch.

The Three T's

Complete each sentence with **there**, **their**, or **they're**.

Please put the flowers _____ .

Have you been _____ before?

_____ going to the zoo tomorrow.

Have you seen _____ new car?

I like swimming in pools when _____ not too crowded.

Your pencil is over _____ on the desk.

_____ house is right next to ours.

Will you go _____ with me?

On Saturday, _____ having a birthday party.

I just saw _____ new lizard.

BRAIN BOX

The three words *there*, *their*, and *they're* are often mixed up.

There tells where something is. Example: Put it over **there**.

Their means *belonging to them*. Example: That is **their** puppy.

They're is a contraction that means *they are*. Example: **They're** the best team.

Now write one sentence for each T-word.

they're _____

_____

there _____

_____

their _____

_____

The Wonderful W's

Complete each sentence with **where**, **were**, or **we're**.

I don't know _____ we are going on our vacation.

If _____ late, he won't let us in.

What _____ you buying in that store?

Tomorrow, _____ going to canoe on the lake.

Do you remember _____ Kelly said we should meet her?

We _____ in Florida last winter.

_____ not singing in the school concert this year.

_____ is your new bicycle?

Do you remember _____ you left your coat?

They _____ the winning team in the relay race.

Where, were, and we're

Now write one sentence for each W-word.

| where | _____ |

_____

| were | _____ |

_____

| we're | _____ |

_____

BRAIN BOX

Where tells or asks about a place. Example: **Where** is your house?

Were is the past tense of *are*. Example: We **were** going there yesterday.

We're is a contraction meaning *we are*. Example: **We're** leaving now.

Double Meanings

Name the **homograph**.

wave

- to move your hand in a greeting
- a body of water that curls and breaks on the shore

Homographs

- a piece of cloth worn around the neck
- when the score of a game is the same for both teams

- a device you wear on your wrist that tells time
- to look at something

- to move oars through water to steer a boat
- a line of objects, like seats in a theater

- one of the four seasons
- to jump suddenly upward

- a symbol of the alphabet
- something you write and mail to someone

- a flying mammal
- something you hit a ball with

Bonus! Choose a pair of homographs and use both meanings in one sentence.

_____

_____

_____

Brain Quest Grade 3 Workbook

BRAIN BOX

Homographs are words that are spelled the same and sound the same but have different meanings.

You Said It

Fix the punctuation in each sentence by adding **quotation marks**.

Kevin said, "Let's go to the zoo tomorrow."

Is that your new dress? asked Chitra.

Quotation marks

Here we are at last! said Ari. I can't wait to see this movie!

I'm cooking spaghetti for dinner, said Rudi's father.

David asked, Why are you laughing so hard?

There was one third grader, said the teacher, who got every answer right.

You'd better wear your coat. It's very cold today, said Philip's grandfather.

BRAIN BOX

Quotation marks show what a person is saying. They go before the first word and after the final punctuation of the quotation. The first word of a quotation is always capitalized.

I'm having my birthday party at the bowling alley, said Carlo.

Are you going to play soccer this year? asked Li.

For example: Leslie said, "We are going to camp this summer."

Watch out! There's a car coming! yelled Alan.

On the Mark!

Add the correct **punctuation mark** to the end of each sentence.

My new dog has one black ear.

What time is your piano lesson

Where did you put your boots

That is so exciting

Julia and Jeffrey both live in North Carolina

Hurry, the bathtub is overflowing onto the floor

Oh no, our dinner is burning

How long will you be gone

That is so wonderful

BRAIN BOX

Declarative sentences are statements that tell about something. They end with a period. For example: I went fishing.

Interrogative sentences are questions that ask about something. They end with a question mark. For example: Do you have a bike?

Exclamatory sentences express strong feelings. They end with an exclamation point. For example: I hooked a big one!

Now write three sentences of your own— one **declarative**, one **interrogative**, and one **exclamatory**. Remember to use correct punctuation.

_____

_____

_____

_____

_____

_____

To the Letter

Add the missing **commas** and **periods** to this letter.

January 14, 2023

Dear Hernando,

I am so excited. We are now in our new home in Middletown Pennsylvania Our kitchen has a new stove refrigerator microwave and sink I have my own bedroom with a nice view

Middletown is a lot smaller than Philadelphia Pennsylvania where we used to live It is so different living in a smaller town

I can't wait to see you at camp this summer We'll sail boats go horseback riding swim and play tennis I hope we'll be in the same tent like we were last year!

Your friend
Neel

Neel McFadden
1234 Main Street
Middletown PA 10001

Hernando Green
9876 1st Street
Philadelphia PA 19100

BRAIN BOX

Commas are used to separate words in a list of three or more things. For example: My favorite fruits are apples, peaches, pears, and bananas.

Commas are used in dates to separate the date from the year. For example: He was born on June 3, 1774.

Commas are used to separate the name of a city and a state. For example: There was a fair in Chicago, Illinois.

Ben's Broken Keyboard

The Shift key on Ben's keyboard is broken, so he couldn't capitalize any words in his homework.

Circle each word that should begin with a **capital letter**.

i watched the red sox play against the yankees last night.

sashiko lives in the united states, but she was born in japan.

is your uncle fred coming to your house for thanksgiving?

we swam in the pacific ocean on our vacation last year.

i can't wait for school to start in september.

can you help me find ms. heather?

chris was born in dallas.

we are going to disneyland on friday.

BRAIN BOX

Always use a capital letter at the beginning of every sentence. Always **capitalize** proper nouns that name a specific person, place, date, holiday, or event.

Sort the **proper nouns** from the sentences above and write them on the cards.

Person

_____
_____
_____
_____

Place

_____
_____
_____
_____
_____

Thing

_____
_____
_____
_____

READING

Do you prefer reading fiction or nonfiction? Do you have a favorite genre? I like reading myths, fairy tales, biographies, and books about history. Let's check out the different kinds of texts in this section!

PARENTS In this section, your child will practice key reading comprehension skills: cause and effect, sequencing, identifying key ideas and details, and more. Developing these skills gives learners the tools they need to be independent and enthusiastic readers.

PLACE A STICKER HERE

For additional resources, visit www.BrainQuest.com/grade3

An Indigenous Peoples' Myth

Read the **story**.

Coyote and the River

It was a beautiful day, and the sun was shining brightly. It was so lovely outdoors that Coyote decided to take a walk. Before long, though, Coyote began to feel hot. "I wish there was a cloud in the sky," said Coyote.

In time, a cloud appeared in the sky and made some shade for Coyote. "Just one cloud doesn't help me feel cooler," he said. "I wish there was more shade."

Soon there were more clouds, and the sky began to darken and look stormy. But Coyote was still hot. He wished for a way to become even cooler.

Suddenly, a small sprinkle of rain came down from the clouds. "I want much more rain," Coyote demanded. Before long, buckets of rain began to fall.

"That's better, but I wish I had a way to cool off my feet," Coyote said. In no time at all, a creek sprang up right beside him. Coyote waded in and cooled off his feet. "I wish the creek was deeper," he said.

All at once, the creek turned into a large, swirling river. Coyote was swept up by the water and nearly drowned. Frightened and sputtering, he was finally tossed onto a bank of this mighty river. Coyote was no longer hot, but he was very wet.

And that is how the Columbia River was created.

Fill in each missing **cause** and **effect**.

Cause		Effect
It was a beautiful day.	→	Coyote decided to go for a walk.
Coyote wanted more shade.	→	
Coyote was still hot.	→	
	→	The rain became heavy.
	→	A creek sprang up right beside Coyote.
Coyote wished that the creek were deeper.	→	

Cause and effect

BRAIN BOX

Cause is the reason why something happens.

Effect is what happens.

A History

Read this **biography** about Hatshepsut.
A biography is a true story about a person's life.

Remembering
facts and
details

The Pharaoh Queen

Around the year 1508 BCE, a baby girl was born to Queen Ahmose, the wife of Pharaoh Tuthmosis I. The pharaoh was the supreme ruler of ancient Egypt, which at the time was a powerful and wealthy empire. Queen Ahmose named her daughter Hatshepsut (hat-SHEP-sut), a name that meant "the foremost of noble ladies."

Young Hatshepsut lived in a palace and had many servants to care for her. During the day she played and sometimes visited her father's private zoo. As she grew older, Hatshepsut attended dinner parties with her parents, where the guests were entertained by dancers, musicians, and acrobats. She also took part in religious festivals and watched special processions (ceremonial marches) from the palace balconies.

When Hatshepsut's father died, her life changed dramatically. She married Tuthmosis II, who was the new pharaoh of Egypt. In time, Hatshepsut, now the Queen of Egypt, gave birth to a daughter, whom she named Neferure. When Tuthmosis II died, his son (Hatshepsut's stepson) became pharaoh . . . even though he was only three years old! Because he was too young to lead, Hatshepsut became his coruler. During Hatshepsut's reign of more than twenty years, she directed the building of many monuments, including the great temple complex of Karnak. She also organized trade networks and an ambitious expedition to a land far down the east coast of Africa. When she died, her mummified body was laid to rest in a temple she built in the Valley of the Kings, the royal burial site for pharaohs and other Egyptian rulers.

Answer the questions.

About what year was Hatshepsut born?

_____

What was the meaning of her name?

_____

_____

What was a pharaoh?

_____

_____

What was the name of Hatshepsut's daughter?

_____

How did Hatshepsut become pharaoh?

_____

_____

What was one of Hatshepsut's accomplishments when she was pharaoh?

_____

_____

_____

About how long did Hatshepsut reign as a pharaoh?

_____

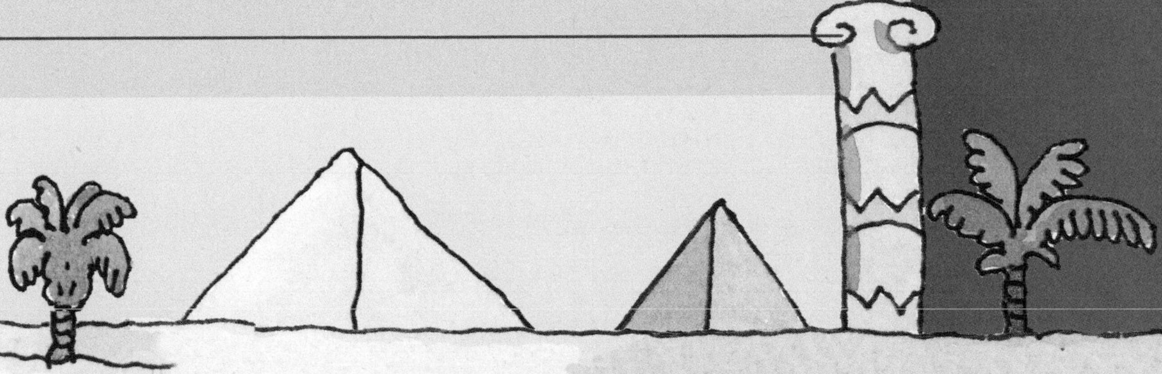

A Rhyming Poem

Read the **poem**.

From "The Duck and the Kangaroo"

By Edward Lear

Said the Duck to the Kangaroo,
"Over the fields, and the water too,
As if you never would stop!
My life is a bore in this nasty pond,
And I long to go out in the world beyond!
I wish I could hop like you!"
Said the Duck to the Kangaroo.

"Please give me a ride on your back!"
Said the Duck to the Kangaroo.
"I would sit quite still, and say nothing but 'Quack,'
The whole of the long day through!
And we'd go to the Dee, and the Jelly Bo Lee,
Over the land, and over the sea;—
Please take me a ride! O, do!"
Said the Duck to the Kangaroo . . .

Said the Kangaroo, "I'm ready!
All in the moonlight pale;
But to balance me well, dear Duck, sit steady!
And quite at the end of my tail!"
So away they went with a hop and a bound,
And they hopped the whole world three times round;
And who so happy,—O who,
As the Duck and the Kangaroo?

Answer the questions.

How does the duck feel about its life in the pond?

_____

What does the duck say he wishes could do like kangaroo?

_____

_____

What does the duck want from the kangaroo?

_____

_____

Where does the kangaroo tell the duck to sit?

_____

_____

Why do you think the duck and the kangaroo felt so happy at the end of the poem?

_____

_____

_____

An African Folktale

Read the **story**.

The Honeybird

Leza was a kind god who wanted the people he had created to have a happy life. That's why he decided to give them three special gourds. "Fly these gourds down to First People," he instructed the honeybird. "Tell them that the red gourd must not be opened. I will <u>descend</u> my spiderweb ladder and meet them on earth to explain its purpose."

The honeybird was eager to know what was inside the gourds. When it reached a clearing near First People's hut, the bird said, "What harm can there be in taking just a tiny peek?" It pecked a hole in the side of the green gourd. Out poured all kinds of seeds. Next, it pecked a hole in the yellow gourd. Out spilled metals, clay, and cloth. Without thinking, it then pecked a hole in the red gourd. Out burst biting insects, poisonous snakes, and rats with sharp teeth.

Just then Leza appeared. He was very angry. "Look what you've done!" he shouted at the honeybird. Leza tried to capture the creatures, but they had hurried away and hidden themselves in dark places.

With great patience, Leza showed First Woman how to plant and care for the seeds in the green gourd. He taught First Man how to make tools from the metals and pots from the clay. He explained how to live with the creatures that had escaped from the red gourd. Then he wished them well and returned to his home in the sky.

First People were alarmed by thoughts of the creatures that they were sure were nearby. "Why should we not live in the sky with Leza?" they asked each other. They began to climb up the spiderweb ladder, but they were too heavy and tumbled back down to earth in a tangle of spider silk.

The honeybird tried to make up for what it had done. Whenever it saw First Man and First Woman, it fluttered its tail feathers and led them with loud chirps to hidden combs of sweet golden honey. Even today, this bird can be heard in the trees where it lives. It calls, "This way! This way!" in hopes that one day it may be forgiven for the trouble it caused.

Answer the questions.

What word best describes the god named Leza?_____
   a. grumpy **b.** curious **c.** kind **d.** frightened

What warning was the honeybird supposed to give to
First People?_____
   a. not to open any of the gourds
   b. not to climb up the spiderweb ladder
   c. not to eat honey
   d. not to open the red gourd

The word *descend* is underlined in paragraph one.
Descend means to _____
   a. go up **b.** hang on to **c.** go down **d.** destroy

Which three things did Leza try to teach First Woman and
First Man after the contents of the red gourd spilled?

_____

_____

Have you ever felt like the honeybird feels in this story?

_____

What made you feel this way?

_____

_____

What do you think is the moral of this story?

_____

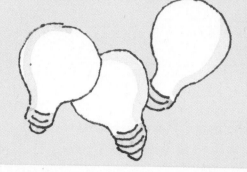

A Biography

Read the **biography**.

Thomas Alva Edison

Young Thomas Edison was naturally curious. He was always asking questions and liked to experiment. Once, when he was very small, he even sat on some goose eggs to see if they would hatch.

As a young boy, Thomas had trouble sitting still in class, so his mother took him out of school and taught Thomas herself at home. He was a fast learner who loved looking for answers in books.

When Thomas was twelve, he started his first job. He sold newspapers, food, and candy on the train that traveled between Port Huron and Detroit. By the time he was fifteen, he was also selling his own weekly paper that he printed himself. It was full of news about the people who traveled or worked on the train.

In 1868, when he was twenty-one, Edison invented an automatic vote counter, for which he received his first patent. (A patent, issued by the United States government, gives an inventor the sole right to make and sell his or her idea.) Unfortunately, the vote counter turned out to be a failure because no one wanted it. Edison vowed that, from that point on, he would invent only things that people wanted. When he was about thirty, Edison established a laboratory in Menlo Park, a small town in New Jersey. It was here that he invented the tinfoil phonograph and the electric light bulb.

Edison was granted over a thousand US patents during his life. As he became increasingly famous, he was called "the Wizard of Menlo Park." Edison felt, though, that his success was the result of hard work, not wizardry. "Genius," he once said, "is one percent inspiration and ninety-nine percent perspiration."

Answer the questions.

Why do you think young Thomas Edison sat on the goose eggs?

_____

What job did Thomas have when he was twelve?

_____

_____

What is a patent?

_____

_____

Why was Edison's automatic vote counter a failure?

_____

_____

What adjective do you think best describes Edison? Why?

_____

_____

Edison said, "Genius is one percent inspiration and ninety-nine percent perspiration." What did he mean when he said this?

_____

_____

Do you agree with Edison's quote about genius? Why or why not?

_____

_____

Get Out the Griddle!

Read the **recipe**.

Patty's Pancakes

INGREDIENTS:

- 4 tablespoons of butter
- 1 cup of flour
- 3 tablespoons of sugar
- a pinch of salt
- 1 tablespoon of baking powder
- 1 cup of milk
- 2 eggs
- $\frac{1}{2}$ teaspoon of vanilla

1. Preheat the griddle to high.
2. Melt 4 tablespoons of butter over low heat on the stove.
3. While the butter is melting, mix the dry ingredients (flour, sugar, salt, and baking powder) together in a large mixing bowl.
4. Mix the wet ingredients (milk, eggs, melted butter, and vanilla) in a second bowl.
5. Slowly pour the wet ingredients into the bowl of dry ingredients and stir about 1 minute.
6. Use a small ladle to pour spoonfuls of batter onto the griddle, making each pancake about 3 inches in diameter.
7. When the top of the pancake starts to bubble, flip the pancake over and cook the other side.
8. The pancakes are done when both sides are brown. Serve them warm with syrup.

Answer the questions about the recipe.

How many tablespoons of butter do you need to melt? _____

What do you need more of: vanilla or baking powder?

_____

Should you start melting the butter before or after you mix
the dry ingredients? _____

**Following
directions**

Does the recipe say how you know when a pancake
is done cooking? _____

Which dry ingredients should be mixed in one bowl?

_____

Which wet ingredients should be mixed in the other bowl?

_____

How long should you stir when you blend the wet and dry
ingredients together? _____

How should the pancakes be served?

_____

What is your favorite meal? List the ingredients you need
to make it.

_____

_____

_____

A Greek Myth

Read the **myth**.

Baucis and Philemon

A long time ago in a town in Greece, there lived a couple who loved each other dearly. Their names were Baucis and Philemon, and they were quite poor. One day, an old beggar appeared at their doorway. He had been turned away by all their neighbors, but when the couple saw him they were filled with pity. "Come inside," they insisted. "We haven't much, but what we have is yours." All they had to eat was a loaf of bread, a few eggs, and a cabbage, but they set a plate before the old man and told him to eat until he was full. They filled his cup with the last bit of pomegranate juice they had. Then, after the old man had finished eating, they wrapped the warmest robe they owned around the old man's shoulders. "We wish there were more to give you," they said, "but, as you can see, we are poor folk. Our cupboards are empty."

"Nay, look again," said the beggar, smiling. Baucis and Philemon, not wishing to offend the old man, opened their cupboards. You can imagine their shock when they saw their cupboards full of all sorts of delicious foods to eat and fresh juices to drink! Before they could say anything, they realized they were no longer dressed in tattered clothes but were wrapped in robes of fine linen. And the house that had only moments before been a hovel was now a great palace all around them. Most surprising of all, though, was the old beggar, for it was Zeus himself, king of all the gods, who stood before them now. "Your eyes do not deceive you," said Zeus. "And for all your kindnesses you shall be rewarded. Ask whatever you want and you shall have your wish."

"We've been poor our whole lives but we've been lucky," they said, "for we have known love. Please grant that we may never have to live one without the other."

The couple lived out the rest of their lives in luxury and never knew hunger again. One day when they had become quite old, they were not at all surprised when suddenly they began to sprout leaves. They embraced each other as their arms became branches, and bark grew around them. "Thank you, Zeus," they said as they turned into trees, for he had granted their wish.

Hundreds of years afterward, people still marveled at the trees, for though one was a linden and the other was an oak, they both grew from a single trunk.

Answer the questions.

What kind of people were Baucis and Philemon? Use at least three adjectives to describe them.

_____

_____

What did Baucis and Philemon offer the old beggar to eat?

_____

_____

Why were Baucis and Philemon shocked?

_____

_____

_____

Why did the couple consider themselves lucky?

_____

_____

_____

What wish did Zeus grant them?

_____

_____

What was so special about the trees?

_____

_____

Remembering details

An Aesop Fable

Read this **fable** by Aesop, a Greek storyteller who lived thousands of years ago. Fables are stories that teach us morals (lessons about life).

A Farmer, His Son, and Their Donkey

One fine day, a farmer and his son were taking their donkey to market. They hoped to sell him for a good price. Before long, they met some women who were collecting water from a well.

"How very silly," said the women. "Those two are trudging along on foot when the donkey could be carrying one of them on its back."

Hearing this, the farmer lifted his boy onto the donkey's back and walked happily along by his son's side.

Presently an old man saw them and cried, "You should be ashamed of yourself, young man. Have you no respect for age? Your father should be riding, and you should be walking!" Red-faced with embarrassment, the son quickly got down and helped his father get up on the donkey.

They had gone only a little further when they came upon a group of young girls. "Have you no sense at all?" They laughed. "Both of you would easily fit on the donkey's back. Why should either one of you have to walk along the dusty road?" Feeling sure they were right, the farmer helped his son get behind him on the donkey's back.

As they neared the market, they met a townsman. "How cruel you are!" he shouted. "That little poor animal has too heavy a load. You two are better able to carry him than he is to carry the two of you." Eager to do the right thing, the two got off the donkey. They tied the donkey's legs together, slung him onto a pole, and strained to carry him on their shoulders as they crossed the bridge near the entrance to the market.

Seeing this strange sight, the townspeople laughed and laughed. In fact, they laughed so loudly that they scared the donkey. The frightened animal kicked off the ropes that bound its legs, fell off the pole, and ran away.

"That will teach you," said an old woman who had followed them. "He who tries to please everyone pleases no one."

Answer the questions.

What is the moral of the story? Describe it in your own words.

_____

_____

Place the pictures in the correct order by numbering them **1** through **5**.
Write a short descriptive caption below each picture.

_____

_____

_____

_____

_____

_____

_____

_____

_____

_____

A Medieval Tale

Read the **story**.

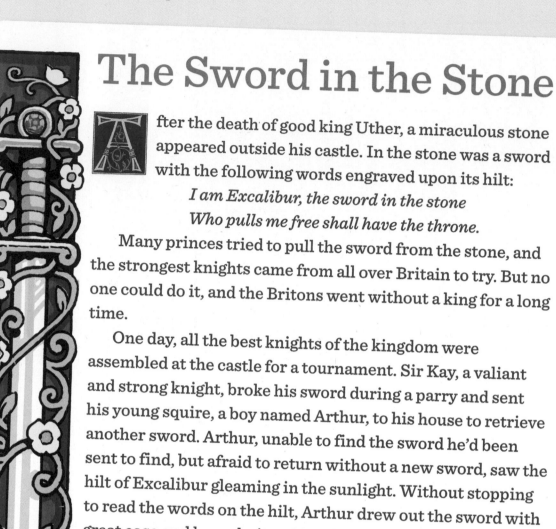

The Sword in the Stone

After the death of good king Uther, a miraculous stone appeared outside his castle. In the stone was a sword with the following words engraved upon its hilt:

I am Excalibur, the sword in the stone
Who pulls me free shall have the throne.

Many princes tried to pull the sword from the stone, and the strongest knights came from all over Britain to try. But no one could do it, and the Britons went without a king for a long time.

One day, all the best knights of the kingdom were assembled at the castle for a tournament. Sir Kay, a valiant and strong knight, broke his sword during a parry and sent his young squire, a boy named Arthur, to his house to retrieve another sword. Arthur, unable to find the sword he'd been sent to find, but afraid to return without a new sword, saw the hilt of Excalibur gleaming in the sunlight. Without stopping to read the words on the hilt, Arthur drew out the sword with great ease and brought it to Sir Kay.

All the knights at the tournament were astonished to see the boy with the sword Excalibur. "Tell us who gave you the sword so that we may proclaim a new king of Britain!" they demanded. When Arthur told them that he had pulled out the great sword himself, they laughed. Sir Kay, seeing the chance to become king, thrust the Excalibur back into the stone and went to retrieve it again, thinking that it would come free easily. But just as it had before, the sword stayed put. All the knights took a turn trying to loosen the sword. When each one of them failed, they brought little Arthur back to see what he could do. Then, before all their eyes, Arthur once again pulled the Excalibur from the stone.

"All hail King Arthur!" the knights proclaimed, and they all pledged their loyalty to the new King of Britain.

What is the name of the sword in the stone? _____

   a. Uther   **b.** Arthur

   c. Excalibur   **d.** Sir Kay

Why is the sword so important?

_____

_____

Why is it strange that Arthur was able to draw the sword from the stone?

_____

_____

Why did Sir Kay put the sword back into the stone? _____

   a. He thought it belonged to him.

   b. He wanted Arthur to take it out again.

   c. He thought it would be easy for him to
       pull back out again.

   d. He didn't want anyone to be king.

How do you think Arthur felt when all the knights hailed him as their king? Why?

_____

_____

_____

_____

On Pointe

Read this **biography** of Misty Copeland.

Misty Copeland

Dancing has been a big part of Misty Copeland's life since she was a kid. Misty's mother was a professional cheerleader who liked dancing around the house to music. She was a single parent, and the family moved a lot. One of six children, Misty was shy and introverted. But she came to see dancing as a way of expressing herself.

At age thirteen, Misty auditioned for the dance team at her school. She would be a dancer, like her mom! The coach told Misty she was very talented and recommended that Misty sign up for ballet classes at a local club.

Many ballerinas start their professional training when they are much younger than thirteen. Though Misty was starting later than most, her teacher told her that she was a prodigy—someone with exceptional talent and abilities. After only about four years of training, Misty was invited to join the American Ballet Theatre (ABT) in New York City as a professional dancer.

Misty encountered negativity and bias as a professional ballet dancer. She was told she was too short, or too muscular, or too brown-skinned to be a ballerina. "[I]t made me really understand the racism in ballet," Misty has said. "I knew that there was no way I could go from being perfect in ballet to all of a sudden, 'I'm a professional but it's no longer right.'" For her first ten years as a professional dancer, Misty was the only Black ballerina at ABT.

Throughout her career, Misty danced in commercials, movies, and videos. In 2014, Misty wrote a memoir about her life. In 2015, she became the first Black woman to be promoted to principal dancer in the ABT. She is one of the world's most accomplished ballet dancers. She has spoken out about the lack of diversity in the world of ballet and the need to provide professional dance training to more children of color.

Number these sentences to show the order in which they happened.

☐ Misty published a memoir about her life.

☐ Misty became the first Black woman to be promoted to principal dancer at the American Ballet Theatre.

☐ Misty auditioned for the dance team at her school.

☐ Misty was invited to join the American Ballet Theatre as a professional dancer.

☐ Misty's coach recommended she sign up for ballet classes at a local club.

102

READING

Remembering
facts and
forming
opinions

A Fairy Tale

Read the **story**.

The Emperor's New Clothes

Many years ago, there lived an emperor who was very vain. He loved to show off his beautiful clothes, and he spent long hours proudly looking at himself in the mirror.

One day, two scoundrels arrived in the kingdom. They came to see the emperor and told him that they could make him a suit of the finest cloth ever imagined. "In fact," they told him, "this cloth will be so delicate that it will appear invisible to anyone who is not smart enough to appreciate it."

The emperor quickly agreed to have this suit made and gave them a large bag filled with gold. The men asked for a loom, the finest silk, and lots of gold thread. They then pretended to begin their work.

Every day, the emperor sent one of his ministers to check on the men's progress. Although they saw that nothing was being made, they were afraid to report this to the emperor. After all, they did not want him to think that they were not smart enough to see and appreciate the cloth. Instead, they told the emperor that his new suit would be magnificent.

At last, the two scoundrels announced that the suit was finished. "Tomorrow will be a holiday, and I will parade through the streets in my new suit," announced the emperor excitedly.

The next morning, the two men pretended to help the emperor put on his new suit. The ministers stood nearby, admiring the work. No one, including the emperor, was willing to admit that what they really saw was the emperor dressed only in his underwear.

The parade began, and crowds of people pushed and shoved to get a good look at the emperor and his new clothes. Because they, too, did not wish to seem less than smart, the people cheered and praised the beauty of his new suit. But then a young boy's voice was heard above the noise of the crowd. "Look," he shouted, "the emperor is wearing no clothes!"

Suddenly, everyone realized that the boy was right. As the crowd laughed and even the ministers chuckled, the foolish emperor rushed back to his palace as fast as he could go. The two scoundrels, of course, were nowhere to be found.

Answer the questions.

In the first paragraph it says that the emperor was very vain.
Circle the best definition of **vain**.

    a. quiet and shy

    b. bold and adventurous

    c. conceited and takes too much pride in his or her looks

    d. smart and clever

What did the two men tell the emperor that they could do?

_____

_____

Why didn't the ministers tell the emperor they saw nothing
being made?

_____

_____

The two men are called scoundrels in this story.
Circle the best definition of **scoundrel**.

    a. someone who likes to do nice things for others

    b. a skilled sewer of clothes

    c. a tricky person who's up to no good

    d. a person who travels from town to town
       looking for work

What lesson do you think the emperor learned from
this experience?

_____

_____

Why do you think the scoundrels played this trick
on the emperor?

_____

_____

Remembering
facts and
forming
opinions

A Science Paper

Read this **essay** about Mars.

Mars, the Red Planet

Dusty, dry, and very, very cold: that's Mars, the fourth planet from the sun. Mars is an average distance of 142 million miles from the fiery center of the universe. Mars is known as the Red Planet because it contains a lot of the chemical iron oxide (also known as rust) in its soil.

Named after the Roman god of war, Mars is about half the size of Earth, but it has twice as many moons. Its two moons, Phobos and Deimos, are irregularly shaped and much, much smaller than Earth's moon.

Besides having twice as many moons as Earth, Mars also has a year that's twice as long: a year on Mars lasts 687 Earth days! (An Earth year is 365 days.) Because it is farther away from the sun, Mars takes longer to orbit, or move, around the sun. A Martian day is about the same length as an Earth day, however: about twenty-four hours. The extra distance from the sun also means that Mars is colder than Earth. At its equator, it is about 68 degrees Fahrenheit, but at its poles temperatures can drop to as low as -220 degrees Fahrenheit! Brrrr!

Mars has both extreme temperatures and extreme landforms. Earth may have some major mountains, but Mars has the highest mountain in our solar system: a volcano called Olympus Mons. This volcano is even taller than Mount Everest—about three times taller!

Though humans haven't yet set foot on Mars, NASA has sent several kinds of spacecraft there to explore since the 1970s. Some, called orbiters, take pictures while they move around the planet. Others, called landers, land on the surface and gather data. Finally, robotic vehicles called rovers touch down and drive around the planet collecting information about what kinds of materials Mars is made of. Scientists are searching for clues life that may have existed billions of years ago, when evidence shows there was water on Mars. Was Mars once a habitable planet? And could it be again?

Answer the questions.

Why is Mars known as the Red Planet?

_____

Is Mars better described as *dry and cold* or *damp and humid*?

_____

What is the name of the tallest mountain in the solar system?

_____

How many moons does Mars have? What are they called?

_____

How long does a year on Mars last?

_____

Name the three kinds of spacecraft NASA has sent to explore Mars over the years.

_____

_____

_____

What are scientists searching for on Mars?

_____

_____

_____

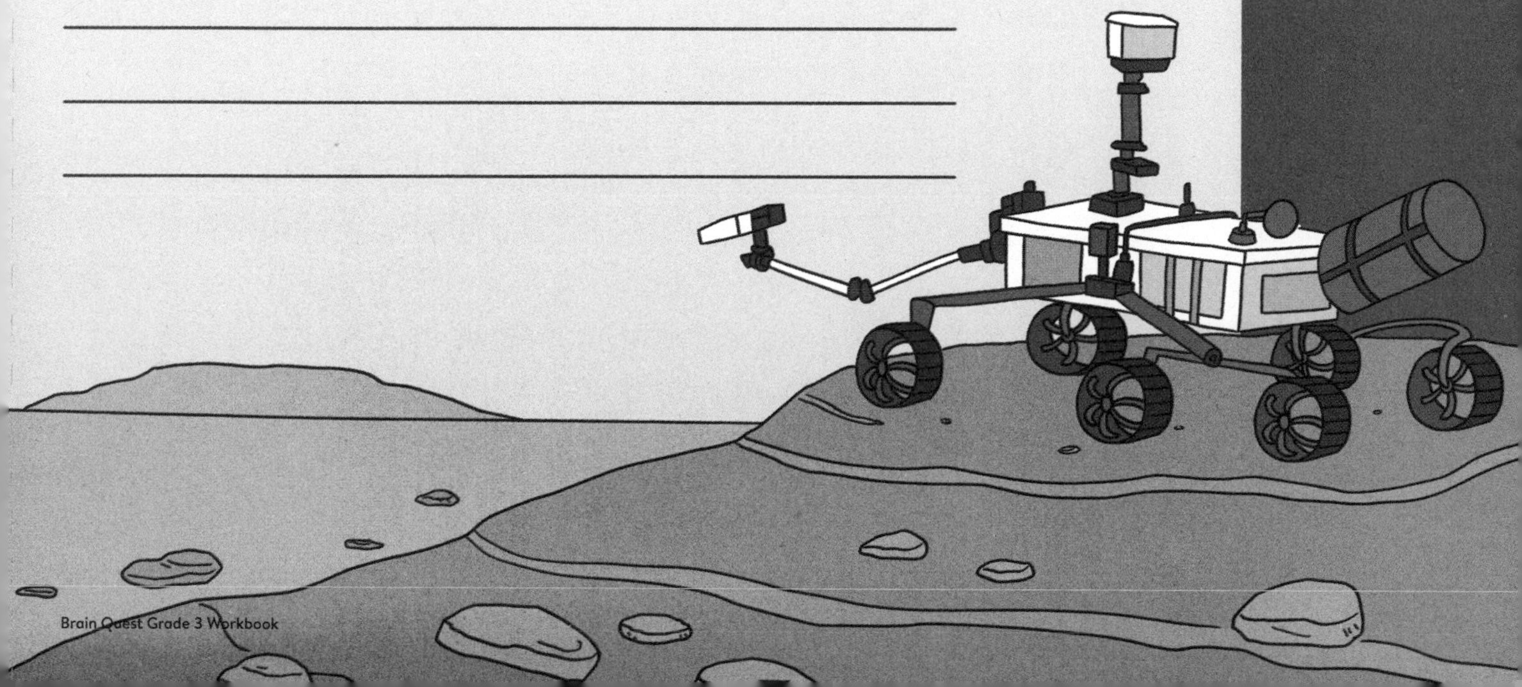

Drawing
conclusions

What Do You Think?

Read each paragraph carefully. Then circle the best **conclusion** based on what you have read.

Mrs. Fussfrot always wears green dresses. She thinks they look wonderful with her green eyes. Yesterday, she went to Belle's Boutique to look for a new dress. They had every color of dress but green.

A Mrs. Fussfrot bought two red dresses.

B Mrs. Fussfrot didn't buy a dress yesterday at Belle's Boutique.

C Mrs. Fussfrot will never go to Belle's Boutique again.

The movie theater, Popcorn Cinema, has 150 seats. Tonight, the movie *Alien Attack* will start at 8:00 p.m. A crowd of 180 people is standing in line for tickets.

A It should be a good movie.

B Everyone will probably buy popcorn.

C Not all the people in line will get a ticket for the 8:00 show.

NOW PLAYING
ALIEN ATTACK

Dr. Drill is a good dentist, but his waiting room is always crowded with patients reading magazines. That's because Dr. Drill is always behind in his schedule. Some patients complain to his receptionist when they become impatient.

A Dr. Drill has very good magazines.

B Dr. Drill has a tiny waiting room.

C If you decide to go to Dr. Drill, you should be prepared to wait.

BRAIN BOX

A **conclusion** is a decision you make after thinking about all the facts you have read.

WRITING

In this section, we'll practice combining sentences, adding details and descriptive words, and organizing paragraphs. Did you know that professional writers spend time doing this kind of work, too? Let's get writing!

PARENTS This section has several writing exercises to inspire your child's critical thinking and guide them to work on long-form writing like essays and stories. Have paper or a notebook ready in case your learner wants to take their creative writing to another page. And don't worry about spelling and grammar—all of this writing is a first draft!

PLACE A STICKER HERE

For additional resources, visit www.BrainQuest.com/grade3

Tell Me More!

Think of **adjectives** and **adverbs** that make each sentence more interesting. Then write a new interesting sentence using these words.

Adding details

The boy ran.
When? Yesterday
How? Very fast
Where? Around the track
Yesterday the boy ran very fast around the track.

The girl played.
When?
What?
Where?

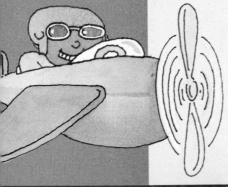

He traveled.
Who?
How?
Why?
When?
Where?

BRAIN BOX

Interesting sentences give details about **when, what, how, why, and where.** For example:

The dog **ran.** The dog **happily ran to the park with his owner.**

Rewrite each sentence by replacing the highlighted verb with a stronger and more specific **verb**.

The three friends played all day long.
The cook washed his pots and pans.
The car drove down the road.

Adding details

Now write your own sentences using the **strong verbs** on the cards.

glisten	_____
	_____

shriek	_____
	_____

whirl	_____
	_____

rejoice	_____
	_____

BRAIN BOX

You can make writing more interesting by using strong verbs that show the action. For example:

The horse **ran**. The horse **galloped**.

Who, what, when, where, and why

Read All About It!

You've been asked to write an article for the school paper. Choose an interesting, exciting, or funny event. Then answer the questions below.

Who was involved in the event?

What was the event and what happened during it?

When did the event take place?

Where did the event take place?

Why was the event interesting, exciting, or funny?

Who?
What?
When?
Where?
Why?

BRAIN BOX

When you write about an event, it is important to answer these questions first:

Who? What? When? Where? Why?

Now use the information from the questions you answered to write your article.

Who, what, when, where, and why

Title

By

Descriptive
writing

Say It with Details

Make the sentences more interesting by thinking of **adjectives** that tell about the highlighted nouns. Then rewrite each sentence using your new adjectives. Remember to change **a** to **an** if your adjective starts with a vowel.

A dragon flew over the forest .

An enormous dragon flew over the
enchanted forest.

The teacher praised the student .

_____

A car drove down the street .

_____

One day the sisters went to a movie .

_____

The man saw a bear .

_____

The boy chased a pig .

_____

The clown wore a wig .

_____

The father baked a cake .

_____

The king lived in a castle .

_____

_____

BRAIN BOX

Adding well-chosen, descriptive **adjectives** to sentences adds detail and interest to writing.

Write a sentence using the word on each card.
Use at least two adjectives per sentence.

WRITING

| magician | The funny magician pulled a cute rabbit out of a hat. |

Descriptive writing

| children | _____ |
| _____ |

| monster | _____ |
| _____ |

| family | _____ |
| _____ |

| party | _____ |
| _____ |

| stranger | _____ |
| _____ |

| lake | _____ |
| _____ |

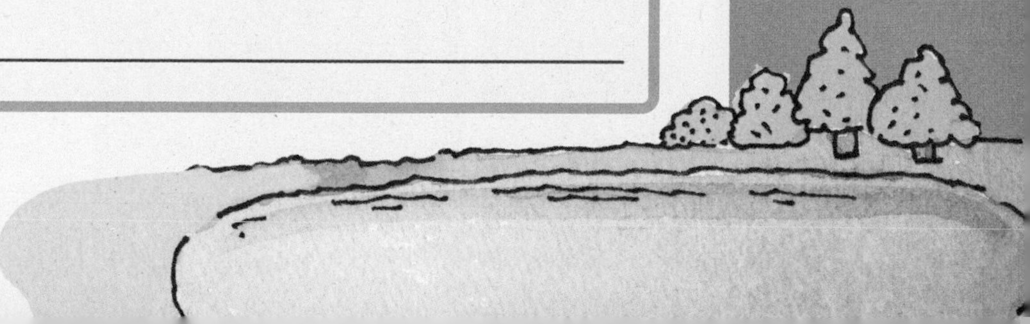

Getting Together

Read each set of sentences. Circle the words that are used more than once. Then **combine** each set of sentences into one sentence, eliminating as many unnecessary words as possible.

When I go to the (pool,) (I will) swim. (I will) also dive off the diving board at the (pool.)

When I go to the pool, I will swim and dive off the diving board.

Everyone was excited. Everyone was having fun.

The boys put on their uniforms. The boys ran out onto the baseball field.

The fans were really excited. The fans at the soccer game cheered loudly for their team.

BRAIN BOX

Combining sentences can make your writing more interesting. Sometimes, one long smooth sentence is better than two or more short sentences that repeat similar information. Often, two sentences with the same subject can be combined into one sentence.

For example:

After school, Levi was tired. Levi was hungry. → After school, Levi was tired and hungry.

Write a paragraph using the topic, ideas, and details in the graphic organizer.

Combining sentences

DETAIL:
The sun was so hot.

DETAIL:
It was nice to cool off in the water.

DETAIL:
The tube was big and made of rubber.

IDEA:
I was glad we went to the water park.

DETAIL:
It wound around the whole waterpark.

IDEA:
We went tubing.

TOPIC:
We had a lot of fun at the water park today.

IDEA:
We floated along the lazy river.

DETAIL:
The tube looked like a giant red doughnut.

IDEA:
We spent time in the giant wave pool.

DETAIL:
The water in the lazy river was warm.

DETAIL:
The wave pool was huge.

DETAIL:
The wave pool was crowded.

What's It All About?

Each of these paragraphs is missing a **topic sentence**, a sentence that introduces the paragraph.

Read each paragraph.

Then write a **topic sentence** for it.

Glow for It!

Some animals glow to attract mates or to communicate with other members of their species. Some glow to distract or scare away predators. And still others, such as the deep-sea anglerfish, glow to lure other animals—their prey—toward them so they can snap them up. These bioluminescent (BI-oh-loo-min-ESS-ent) creatures live in all parts of the ocean, from its surface to its floor. Glowing creatures also live on land. Have you ever seen a firefly? Then you've seen a bioluminescent animal!

Topic Sentence:

_____

_____

_____

Up for the Challenge

Marta made posters encouraging people to recycle. Leo and Damaris hung them all over school. Our assistant principal, Mr. Chen, helped us write an announcement reminding people not to throw away materials, like paper, that can be recycled. And Kwame read the announcement in the cafeteria during lunch. Everyone clapped! We were all happy to do our part.

Topic sentences

Topic Sentence:

_____

_____

_____

Going Camping

Pack a tent, so you have some covering if it rains. A tent can also protect you from bugs and other critters. You should also bring either a sleeping bag or a mat to sleep on top of. Also remember to pack some food to eat—and to bring lots of fresh water! It's good to take a lantern and some extra batteries because many campsites are very dark after sundown. And don't forget your compass! That handy tool can tell you which direction you're headed if you set out on a hike.

Topic Sentence:

_____

_____

Strong Foundations

Read the paragraph. Underline the **topic sentence** in red. Underline the **detail sentences** in blue. Underline the **concluding sentence** in green.

Katie had a great time at tennis practice this morning. First she practiced her forehand shot with her coach. Then she worked on her backhand with the ball machine. Once she was warmed up, Katie and her coach played a few practice games, so she could work on her serve. Katie was exhausted when she got home, but at least she felt ready for Saturday's tournament.

BRAIN BOX

A **paragraph** is a group of sentences that talks about the same main idea. Paragraphs have three parts: a beginning, a middle, and an end.

The **beginning** of a paragraph usually has a topic sentence. It tells what the rest of the paragraph is about.

The **middle** of a paragraph contains details about the main idea.

The **conclusion** of a paragraph usually finishes the main idea of the paragraph.

The first line of every paragraph is indented, which means the first word always begins a little bit to the right of the rest of the lines.

Summer Vacation

Organize the sentences on the cards into paragraphs. Number the sentences in the order that makes the most sense.

Paragraph structure

- [ ] We drove from California to New York.
- [ ] This summer, my family drove across the country for vacation.
- [ ] Along the way, we stopped in small towns and big cities.
- [ ] We had fun in each town and city.

- [ ] I was sad when we had to leave.
- [ ] While we were in Hot Springs, we spent most of our time in the national park.
- [ ] We hiked in the mountains and had a picnic by a creek.
- [ ] My favorite place was Hot Springs, Arkansas.

- [ ] My mom and dad had to be back at work, and I was starting to miss my dog, Baxter.
- [ ] Seven days later, we pulled up in our driveway.
- [ ] After four weeks of touring the United States, it was time to head home.
- [ ] I had a great time, but I was happy to be home.

All About Me

Finish the sentences.

Paragraph 1 Four adjectives that describe me well are:

_____ _____ _____ _____

I live in a/an (describe the place you live)

_____

I live there with

_____

Paragraph 2

My school is called _____

My favorite subject is _____

The best thing about school is _____

Paragraph 3

After school, I like to _____

_____

My hobbies are _____

_____

Before I go to bed each night, I always _____

_____

_____

Use your answers from the previous page to write three paragraphs about yourself. Include a topic sentence, supporting details, and a concluding sentence in each paragraph. Don't forget to indent the first line.

Narrative paragraphs

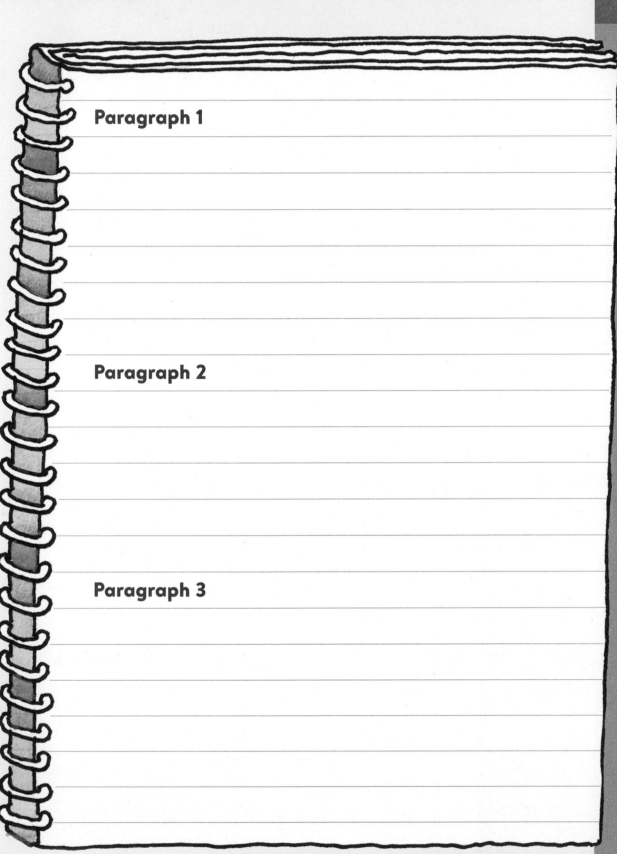

Paragraph 1

Paragraph 2

Paragraph 3

That's the Point!

Read the **persuasive paragraph**.
Then answer the questions.

Running is the most ideal exercise for staying healthy and fit. Unlike many other sports, running is something that just about anyone can do, and it isn't hard to get started. Running also burns calories while giving your heart and legs a great workout. You can either do it with a friend or you can go by yourself. Of course, the best part about running is you can do it anywhere. Whether you're in a gym, on the sidewalk, or at the beach, all you need is a pair of running shoes to get moving. If you've never run before, give it a try. You'll have fun and feel good after you do it!

BRAIN BOX

Persuasive writing tries to get the reader to agree with an opinion or point of view. Persuasive paragraphs contain three elements:

1) A **topic sentence**—a sentence that introduces the opinion

2) **Supporting facts**—details, facts, or reasons that support the opinion

3) A **conclusion**—a sentence that restates the opinion or finishes the argument

What is the main idea of the topic sentence?

_____

Is the main idea a fact or an opinion?

_____

What are some of the reasons the writer gives to support his or her main idea?

_____

_____

_____

_____

_____

_____

Now it's your turn to write a **persuasive paragraph**. First, think about an issue you feel strongly about. Use some of the persuasive words from the colored boxes to strengthen your writing.

necessary	surely	definitely	best
certainly	only	important	amazing

Persuasive paragraphs

Write your opinion about the issue here.

List any facts, details, or reasons that support your opinion here. Be sure to include the details that would most likely convince someone else to agree with your opinions.

Restate your opinion from the top of the page, but express it in a different way.

Persuasive
paragraphs

Here's My Point!

Now, take your answers from the questions on the previous page and organize them into your own **persuasive paragraph**.

Make sure you state your case clearly in your topic sentence, use the middle of the paragraph to support your opinion, and conclude by restating your opinion or finishing the argument.

All About Outlines

Read this **outline** for a short report about Halloween. Use the paragraph ideas in the boxes to help you fill in the blanks.

Making a jack-o'-lantern	Knocking on doors
Making a costume	How Halloween started

I. Paragraph 1—Introduction:

a. When Halloween is celebrated

b. Where Halloween is celebrated

c.

d. Halloween traditions

Using outlines

II. Paragraph 2—Costumes:

a. Costume ideas

b.

c. Buying a costume

III. Paragraph 3—Pumpkins:

a. Pumpkin picking

b.

c. Roasting pumpkin seeds

BRAIN BOX

An **outline** usually contains a list of ideas grouped together in the same order they will be presented in a report. Outlines are often broken down by paragraphs. Creating an outline is a great way to organize your thoughts before writing the report.

IV. Paragraph 4—Trick-or-Treating:

a. Getting dressed

b.

c. Sorting candy

Time to Outline

Write an outline for a short report about your favorite holiday.

Using outlines

I. Paragraph 1—Introduction:

a.

b.

c.

II. Paragraph 2—Main Idea:

a.

b.

c.

When writing a report, think about what details to include. What points do you want to make? What facts are especially interesting?

III. Paragraph 3—Main Idea:

a.

b.

c.

IV. Paragraph 4—Main Idea:

a.

b.

c.

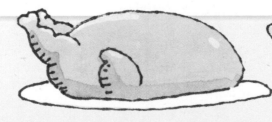

Now use your outline to write a short report about your favorite holiday. Expand on the ideas you listed by using interesting language and details in your writing.

My Favorite Holiday:

What's Your Line?

There are many kinds of **poetry**. Some poems have words that rhyme and some don't. Some poems are serious and some are playful.

Here's a short nonsense poem that ends with words that rhyme. Each line of this poem has five beats.

There once was a snake
Who liked to eat cake

Write a line with five beats to finish each of these poems. Use the Word Boxes below if you need ideas for rhyming words.

There once was a goat
who rode in a boat.

There once was a flea
_____

There once was a cat
_____

There once was a crow
_____

boat	bee	bat	blow
coat	ski	brat	doe
vote	flee	chat	dough
float	pea	fat	flow
wrote	knee	flat	go

You Name It!

Write an **acrostic poem** using the letters in your name.

Poetry

Hello, My Name is
Fred

BRAIN BOX

Acrostic poetry uses the letters of a name to begin each line in the poem.
For example:

Fred

Friendly and fun
Red hair
Energetic
Dynamic

The Proof Is in the Writing

Study the chart to learn how to use **proofreading marks**.

Symbol	What it means	Example
a (capitalize mark)	capitalize	The pacific Ocean is the largest ocean in the world.
A (make lowercase mark)	make lowercase	There are 25,000 Islands scattered throughout the ocean.
∧	insert letter to spell correctly	The Pacific Ocean is so wide it touches the coasts of Indonesia and Colobia. (∧m)
⸮ (caret with comma)	add a comma	It is home to incredible whales, sharks, and coral reefs.
⊙	add a period	The Pacific Ocean gets its name from the word for peaceful⊙ It isn't always peaceful, though.
ℐ (delete mark)	delete or take out	The area the Pacific Ocean covers is ~~bigger~~ larger than the area covered by all the dry land on Earth.
¶	start a new paragraph	The Pacific Ocean has the deepest trenches in the world.¶ The Indian Ocean is another beautiful ocean.

BRAIN BOX

Proofreading marks are used to edit a piece of writing. They are a handy way of marking errors for review or revision.

Use **proofreading marks** to mark the errors in this essay. Use a red pen.

If you travel to hawaiʻi, don't forget to vsit the Mauna Loa Volcano. Mauna Loa is the the biggest Volcano on earth, and one of the most active Tourists visit from all over the World to see hot red lava flowing from the volcano down into the Pacific Ocean below.

Mauna Loa is located on the the island of Hawaiʻi, and it is part of Hawaiʻi Volcanoes National park. The park is so big that it could take you several days just to drive arund and see all the sights. Be sure to pack your raincoat and boots, because it's often cool and cloudy rainy at the top of the volcino. Of course as soon as you drive down to sea level the weather gets warmer and sunnier that's Hawaiʻi!

PROFESSIONAL PROOFREADING TIP!
The ʻokina in "Hawaiʻi" looks like a right-facing apostrophe. It indicates a clean break between vowels.

Writing a Journal Entry

Pick one of the following writing prompts and write a **journal entry** about it.

1. Describe something that makes you feel excited and nervous at the same time. Why do you think you have both these feelings about this thing?

2. What is something you want to learn how to do? What is one way you could begin to learn this new skill?

3. Write about a special day. What did you do? Where did you go?

BRAIN BOX

A writing **prompt** is a suggested topic, idea, or starting point for a piece of writing.

MATH SKILLS

Dad shouts, "Come inside in five minutes!" or your brother asks, "Can you share your grapes?" Measuring time, dividing a snack into equal parts—you use math all the time! Let's turn the page and build our math skills.

PARENTS This section features key third-grade math concepts: place value, estimation, 3D shapes, charts and graphs, and more. Understanding estimation leads children to develop mental math dexterity, and the ability to reason with numbers is key to lifelong mathematical success.

How Very Odd

Circle the **even** numbers. Draw a square around the **odd** numbers.

Odd
and even
numbers

4	9	0	2	17	12	99
146	239	28	70	501	34	23
39	18	301	55	87	164	101
219	500	989	998	3	25	744

Fill in the missing numbers. Then circle all the even numbers and draw a square around the odd numbers.

8 ___ ___ 11 12 ___ 14 ___ ___ ___ 18

BRAIN BOX

An **even** number is a whole number that ends in **0, 2, 4, 6,** or **8.**

An **odd** number is a whole number that ends in **1, 3, 5, 7,** or **9.**

When you add two even numbers, the answer is always even.

When you add two odd numbers, the answer is always even.

When you add one odd number and one even number, the answer is always odd.

Circle the correct answer.

When you add 34 and 18, two even numbers, the sum will be

odd   even

When you add 25 and 13, the sum will be

odd   even

When you add 21 and 42, the sum will be

odd   even

Number Riddles

Solve the puzzles about **odd** and **even** numbers.

What even, 2-digit number is larger than 2 but smaller than 12?

10

What even number is greater than 6 and less than 18, and can be divided evenly by 6?

What odd number between 16 and 34 can be evenly divided by 5?

What odd number between 9 and 21 can be evenly divided by 3?

What even 2-digit number is smaller than 46, larger than 20, and a multiple of 9?

What odd 2-digit number between 20 and 30 has digits that add up to 7?

What even 3-digit number between 75 and 150 has digits that add up to 1?

What odd 3-digit number has digits that are all the same and that add up to 9?

What's Its Value?

Answer the following questions about place value.

Place value

What is the place value of the digit 9 in the number 5,921?

hundreds

In the number 52,689, which digit is in the ten-thousands place?

_____

What is the place value of the digit 6 in the number 86,542?

_____

Which digit is in the tens place in the number 34,720?

_____

Write the number seventy thousand, two hundred and eight.

_____

BRAIN BOX

You can use place value to figure out how much each digit is worth.
For example: **423,879**

hundred-thousands	ten-thousands	thousands	hundreds	tens	ones
4	2	3	8	7	9

The **4** tells us there are **4** hundred-thousands. The **2** tells us there are **2** ten-thousands. The **3** tells us there are **3** thousands. The **8** tells us there are **8** hundreds. The **7** tells us there are **7** tens. The **9** tells us there are **9** ones. This number is pronounced **four hundred twenty-three thousand, eight hundred seventy-nine.**

Place value

What is the place value of the digit 3 in the number 526,310?

_____

Write the number that has 2 hundred-thousands, 7 ten-thousands, 7 thousands, 5 hundreds, 3 tens, 9 ones.

_____

Which digit is in the hundreds place in the number 59,216?

_____

Write the number seventy-five thousand, two hundred, twenty-two.

_____

What is the place value of the digit 4 in the number 34,890?

_____

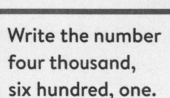

Write the number four thousand, six hundred, one.

_____

In the number 305,678, which digit is in the hundred-thousands place?

_____

Write the number 48,567 using words.

_____

_____

Count Them Up

Answer the following questions about numbers. Use the extra space on the cards to do your calculating. Write the correct answer in the box on the card.

Number sense

How many zeros does the number seven thousand, seven have?

7,007   2

I have seventy ones. What number am I?

I have eighty hundreds. What number am I?

How many zeros does the number one hundred thousand, ten have?

How many digits are in the number seven hundred thousand?

What number is the same as sixteen tens?

How many digits are in the number eighty one thousand?

I have ten tens and three ones. What number am I?

How many zeros does the number ten thousand, fifty have?

What's My Line?

Identify each of these figures. Write **line**, **ray**, or **line segment** in the space beside the figure.

Lines, line segments, and rays

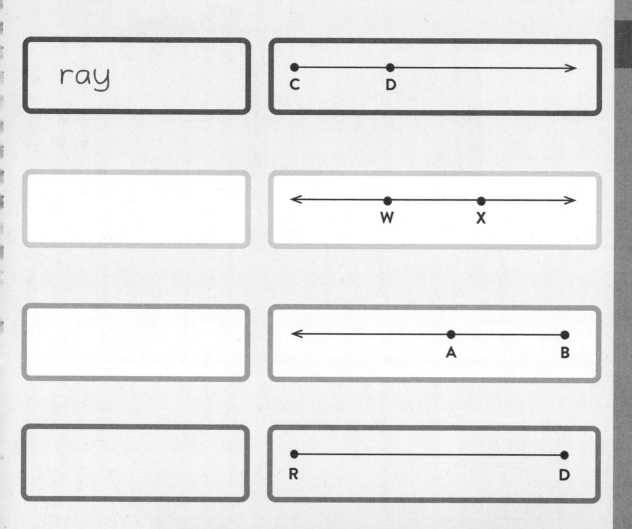

ray

C   D →

←—— W   X ——→

←—— A   B

R ——————— D

BRAIN BOX

A **line** goes on and on in both directions forever. It is named by any two points (dots that show a certain location) on the line. For example:

←——•——•——→ = **line GH** or **line HG**
    G   H

A **ray** has only one end point and continues on and on in the other direction. It is always named starting with its one end point. For example:

•——•————→ = **ray ST**
S   T

A **line segment** is part of a line that stops at both ends. A line segment is named by a point at each end, called an end point. For example:

•———————• = **line segment MN** or **line segment NM**
M   N

What's Your Angle?

Identify each of these angles by writing **right**, **acute**, or **obtuse** on the line below the angle.

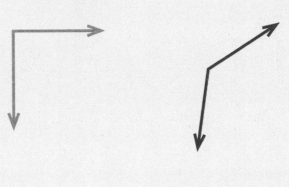

acute
_____   _____   _____

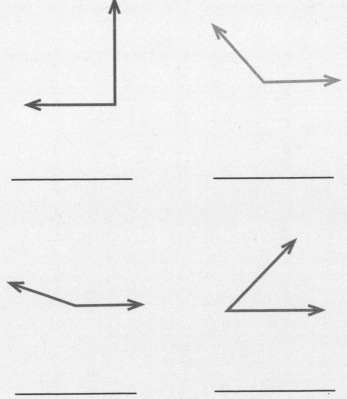

_____   _____

_____   _____

BRAIN BOX

When two lines meet at one point they form an **angle**.

This is angle A.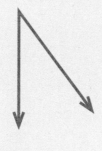

Angles can be different sizes. Some are wide and some are narrow.

A **right angle** forms a square corner.

An **acute angle** is less than a right angle.

An **obtuse angle** is greater than a right angle.

Angles

How many angles does a triangle have?

_____

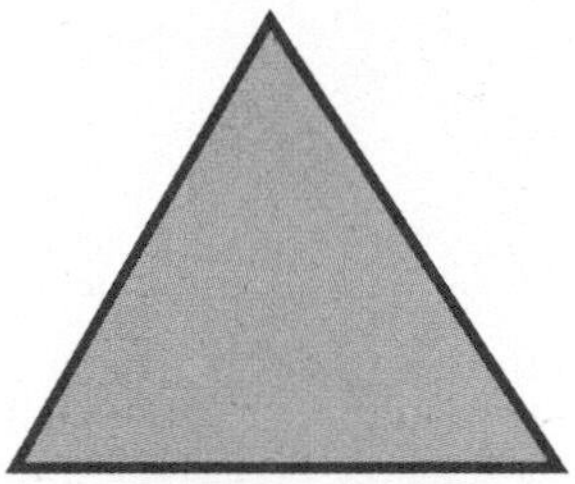

How many angles does an octagon have?

_____

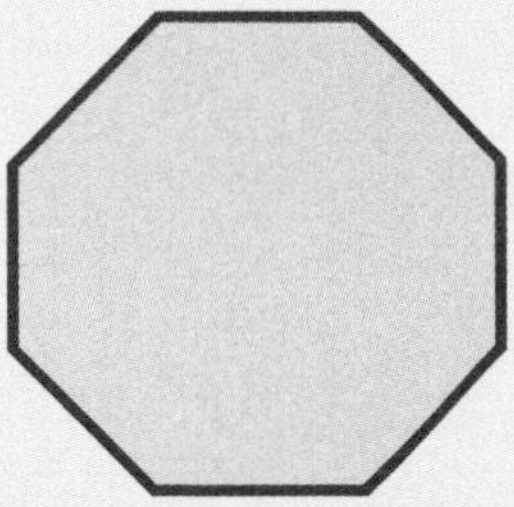

How many angles does a rectangle have?

_____

Does a square have acute, right, or obtuse angles?

_____

Draw an **acute angle**, a **right angle**, and an **obtuse angle** in the spaces below. Label each.

_____

_____

_____

142

Shape Up

Draw a line to match each **solid figure** to its name.

Three-
dimensional
geometric
figures

sphere

cube

rectangular prism

cylinder

cone

BRAIN BOX

Three-dimensional or **3D** figures are often called solid figures.

A **sphere** is a **3D** circle.

A **cube** is a **3D** square.

A **rectangular prism** is a **3D** rectangle.

A **cylinder** is a **3D** figure with circles at either end.

A **cone** is a **3D** figure with a circle at one end and a point at the other end.

What shape is each side of a cube? _____

What shape is the flat side of a cone? _____

How many faces does a rectangular prism have? _____

Three-dimensional geometric figures

Circle the one that does not belong in this group:

cone, cylinder, cube, sphere, triangle

Why doesn't it belong?

_____

How many angles does a sphere have? _____

What solid figure are dice? _____

How many flat faces does a cylinder have? _____

What shape is the top and the bottom of a cylinder?

_____

Which solid figure is a bongo drum: a cylinder, a cube, a cone, or a rectangular prism? _____

What solid figure is a baseball? _____

BRAIN BOX

The flat sides of a 3D figure are called **faces.**

What's Next?

What comes next in each of these **patterns**?
Draw your answer in the box.

Identifying
patterns

What two letters come next in each of
these patterns?

A b c D e f G h i J k l M n _____ _____

z y x w v u t s r q p o _____ _____

a c e g i k m o q _____ _____

a z b y c x d w e v f u g t _____ _____

What two numbers come next in each of these series?

11   22   33   44   55   66   _____   _____

4   44   444   4,444   _____   _____

7   14   21   28   35   _____   _____

25   50   75   100   125   _____   _____

1   3   2   4   3   5   4   6   5   _____   _____

2   3   5   8   12   17   _____   _____

4   3   7   6   10   9   13   _____   _____

Identifying patterns

BRAIN BOX

To figure out the pattern for a number series, look at the relationship between each number and the number that follows it in the series.

For example:

2   5   3   6   4   7   5

+3   −2   +3   −2   +3   −2

The pattern for this number series is (+ 3, − 2). The next two numbers would be **8** and **6**.

Round 'Em Up

Round these numbers to the nearest **ten**. If you round up, draw a circle around your answer. If you round down, draw a box around your answer.

Rounding numbers

58    11 _____   26 _____   83 _____

62 _____   37 _____   44 _____   79 _____

17 _____   74 _____   19 _____   24 _____

Round these numbers to the nearest **hundred**. If you round up, draw a circle around your answer. If you round down, draw a box around your answer.

833 | 800 | 487 _____   729 _____   596 _____

924 _____   297 _____   678 _____   354 _____

324 _____   198 _____   109 _____   247 _____

429 _____   888 _____   949 _____   151 _____

BRAIN BOX

Rounding to the nearest ten

If the digit in the ones place is 5 or greater, **round up** to the **nearest ten**. If the digit in the ones place is 4 or less, **round down** to the nearest ten.

66 rounds up to 70.

64 rounds down to 60.

Rounding to the nearest hundred

If the digit in the tens place is 5 or greater, **round up** to the **nearest hundred**. If the digit in the tens place is 4 or less, **round down** to the nearest hundred.

251 rounds up to 300.

249 rounds down to 200.

. . . and Up!

Now try rounding with larger numbers.

The tallest mountain on Earth is Mauna Loa, a volcano in Hawai'i. From its base to its peak, it stands more than 56,000 feet high. Round 56,000 to the nearest ten thousand.

Did you think Mount Everest was the tallest? Nope! From its base to its peak, Mount Everest is 29,032 feet tall. Round 29,032 to the nearest thousand.

BRAIN BOX

Rounding numbers makes them easier to work with, especially when you have to do calculations in your head. For example, if you are at the grocery store, rounding numbers to the nearest dollar as you shop can tell you about how much your total will be.

Mauna Loa's base is sunk deep into the Pacific Ocean floor, so we can't see the 42,650 feet of it below water. Round 42,650 to the nearest ten thousand.

The deepest spot on Earth can be found in the Pacific Ocean. Challenger Deep, in the Mariana Trench, is 36,201 feet deep. Round 36,201 to the nearest ten thousand.

On the continent of Africa stretches Earth's longest river. The Nile flows from south to north for 4,132 miles. Round 4,132 to the nearest thousand.

Close Enough

Estimate the sums and differences by rounding each number to the nearest ten.

MATH SKILLS

Estimating in number operations

$\begin{array}{r} 77 \rightarrow 80 \\ + \ 24 \ + \ 20 \\ \hline 100 \end{array}$

$\begin{array}{r} 59 \\ + \ 67 \\ \hline \end{array}$

$\begin{array}{r} 91 \\ - \ 26 \\ \hline \end{array}$

$\begin{array}{r} 98 \\ - \ 67 \\ \hline \end{array}$

$\begin{array}{r} 62 \\ + \ 21 \\ \hline \end{array}$

$\begin{array}{r} 41 \\ + \ 27 \\ \hline \end{array}$

$\begin{array}{r} 88 \\ + \ 11 \\ \hline \end{array}$

$\begin{array}{r} 38 \\ + \ 25 \\ \hline \end{array}$

$\begin{array}{r} 66 \\ - \ 11 \\ \hline \end{array}$

$\begin{array}{r} 73 \\ - \ 28 \\ \hline \end{array}$

$\begin{array}{r} 51 \\ - \ 43 \\ \hline \end{array}$

$\begin{array}{r} 87 \\ - \ 39 \\ \hline \end{array}$

BRAIN BOX

To **estimate** means to find an answer that is close enough to the right answer, usually by making calculations.

One way to estimate is to use **rounding**.

For example: **87 + 72**

Using rounding, this problem becomes 90 + 70, which equals 160.

This tells you that the answer to 87 + 72 will be close to 160.

Estimate the sums and differences by rounding each number to the nearest hundred.

Estimating in number operations

876 → 900 + 211 → + 200 ——— 1100	859 + 611	729 + 229
558 + 307	285 + 198	727 + 254
651 + 495	504 + 386	437 + 109
828 + 751	939 + 621	727 + 158

Gone Fishing

Felix Flounder goes fishing every weekend from May through October. The **bar graph** shows how many fish he caught each month.

Use the bar graph to answer the questions.

Reading a bar graph

In which month did Felix catch the most fish? _____

How many fish did Felix catch in June? _____

In which month did Felix catch the fewest fish? _____

How many more fish did Felix catch in July than he did in June? _____

How many fish did Felix catch in May and June combined? _____

Show and Tell

The third graders at Dwight Elementary School made a **graph** showing how many of them own particular kinds of pets.

Use the graph to answer the questions.

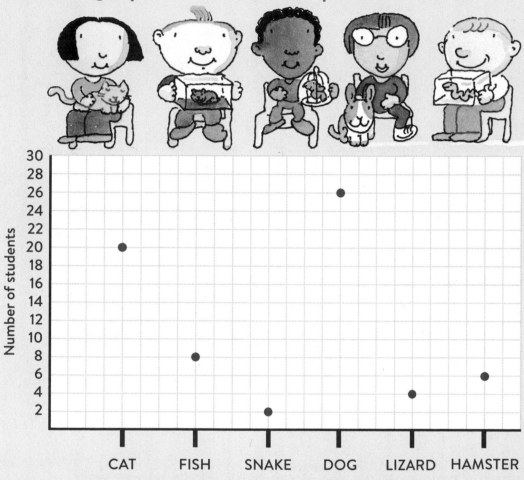

How many third graders own fish? _____

What kind of pet is owned by the greatest number of students? _____

What kind of pet is owned by the fewest number of students? _____

How many third graders own snakes? _____

Do more students own hamsters or lizards? _____

How many more third graders own dogs than cats? _____

Muscleville Medals

Muscleville High School made a **chart** of all the medals they have won in the state sport championships.

Use the chart to answer the questions.

Events	GOLD	SILVER	BRONZE
speed swimming events	3	4	2
diving events	5	5	2
relay races	2	4	1
running races	0	6	4
balance beam events	2	3	3
high and low jumps	1	5	0
hurdle races	4	4	3

How many gold medals did Muscleville High win in all? _____

How many silver medals did they win in all? _____

How many bronze medals did they win in all? _____

In what kind of events did they win the most medals? _____

In what kind of events did they win the fewest medals? _____

How many silver medals did they win in relay races and running races combined? _____

In what kind of events did they win the most gold medals? _____

First Things First

Solve each problem. Show your work.

$(6 + 4) \times 4 =$ __40__

$(10) \times 4$

Math with
multiple steps

$27 \div (4 + 5) =$ _____

$(3 + 2) \times (8 - 1) =$ _____

$(4 \times 7) \div 4 =$ _____

$(9 \div 3) - 3 =$ _____

$8 + (14 \div 2) =$ _____

$(8 - 2) + (6 - 3) =$ _____

$4 + (8 \times 7) =$ _____

BRAIN BOX

Sometimes you have to solve a
math problem that involves more
than one step. Always solve the
part or parts in parentheses first.
Then solve the rest of the problem.

Impress Your Friends

Do these mathematical tricks. Learn the steps by heart so you can amaze your friends.

The Number One Math Trick!

1. Pick a number from 1 to 100.

2. Multiply that number by 2.

3. Now add 2.

4. Next divide by 2.

5. Subtract the original number from the result of Step 4.

6. The number is always 1!

The Magic Number Nine!

1. Write down your phone number without the dash or area code.

2. Arrange the digits to make the largest number possible.

3. Arrange the digits to make the smallest number possible.

4. Subtract the smaller number from the larger number.

5. Add up all the digits of the result.

6. Now add the two digits you ended up with.

7. The answer is 9!

ADDITION AND SUBTRACTION

Let's put some of those math concepts we mastered in the last section to use! Time to practice addition and subtraction with three-digit (and greater!) numbers.

PARENTS In this section, learners build on their understanding of place value and apply it to addition and subtraction of larger numbers. Encourage your child to check their answers, ideally using a different addition or subtraction strategy.

PLACE A STICKER HERE

For additional resources, visit www.BrainQuest.com/grade3

Fact Families

Each triangle contains the numbers in a **fact family**.
Write the equations for each fact family.

Fact families

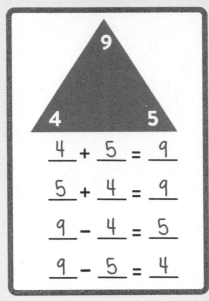

$$\underline{4} + \underline{5} = \underline{9}$$
$$\underline{5} + \underline{4} = \underline{9}$$
$$\underline{9} - \underline{4} = \underline{5}$$
$$\underline{9} - \underline{5} = \underline{4}$$

11 · 2 · 9

___ + ___ = ___
___ + ___ = ___
___ − ___ = ___
___ − ___ = ___

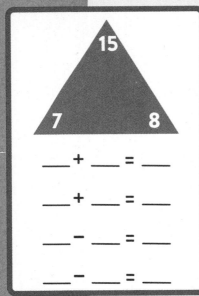

15 · 7 · 8

___ + ___ = ___
___ + ___ = ___
___ − ___ = ___
___ − ___ = ___

8 · 17 · 9

___ + ___ = ___
___ + ___ = ___
___ − ___ = ___
___ − ___ = ___

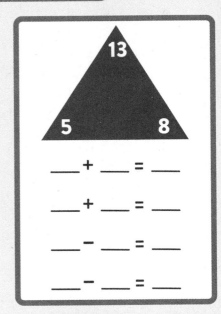

13 · 5 · 8

___ + ___ = ___
___ + ___ = ___
___ − ___ = ___
___ − ___ = ___

BRAIN BOX

A **fact family** is a set of related addition and subtraction equations that use the same numbers. Each fact family has two addition equations and two subtraction equations using the same three numbers.

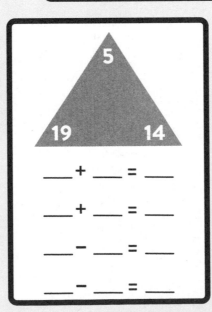

5 · 19 · 14

___ + ___ = ___
___ + ___ = ___
___ − ___ = ___
___ − ___ = ___

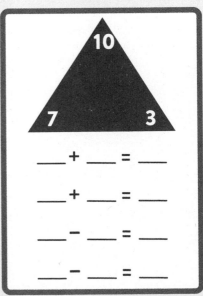

10 · 7 · 3

___ + ___ = ___
___ + ___ = ___
___ − ___ = ___
___ − ___ = ___

Write the equations for each fact family.

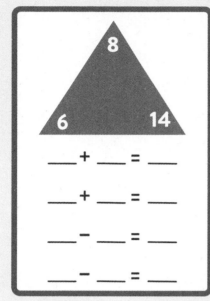

___ + ___ = ___

___ + ___ = ___

___ − ___ = ___

___ − ___ = ___

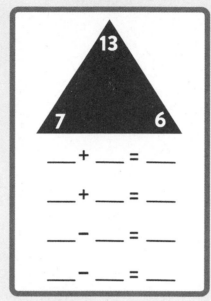

___ + ___ = ___

___ + ___ = ___

___ − ___ = ___

___ − ___ = ___

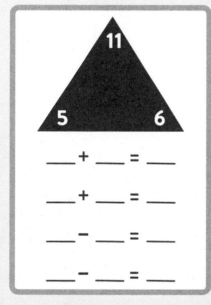

___ + ___ = ___

___ + ___ = ___

___ − ___ = ___

___ − ___ = ___

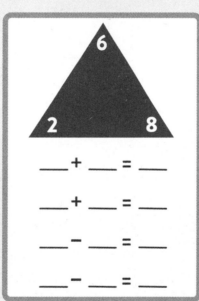

___ + ___ = ___

___ + ___ = ___

___ − ___ = ___

___ − ___ = ___

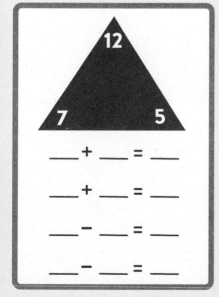

___ + ___ = ___

___ + ___ = ___

___ − ___ = ___

___ − ___ = ___

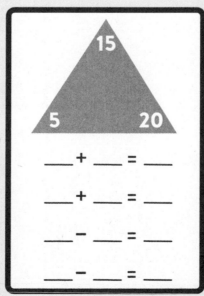

___ + ___ = ___

___ + ___ = ___

___ − ___ = ___

___ − ___ = ___

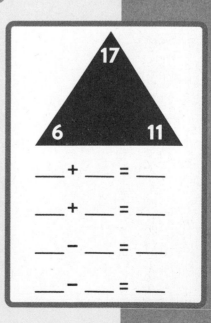

___ + ___ = ___

___ + ___ = ___

___ − ___ = ___

___ − ___ = ___

Does It Add Up?

Add the numbers to find the **sum.**

Addition

```
   37
+  12
_____
```

```
  235
+ 542
_____
```

```
   87
+  11
_____
```

```
  628
+ 171
_____
```

```
   77
+  22
_____
```

```
  625
+ 324
_____
```

```
  354
+ 544
_____
```

```
   65
+  13
_____
```

```
   27
+  61
_____
```

```
  544
+ 323
_____
```

```
  899
+ 100
_____
```

```
  731
+ 247
_____
```

BRAIN BOX

Addition is finding the total when you combine two or more numbers. **Addends** are the numbers being added. The **sum** is the answer to an addition problem.

This is one way to add multidigit numbers: add vertically by place value.

Example: 54 + 23

Step 1: Add the ones.
```
  5 | 4
+ 2 | 3
------
    | 7
```

Step 2: Add the tens.
```
  5 | 4
+ 2 | 3
------
  7 | 7
```

This is another way to add multidigit numbers: add horizontally by place value.

Example: 624 + 315

Step 1: Write each number in **expanded form.**

624 = 600 + 20 + 4
315 = 300 + 10 + 5

Step 2: Add like places

Add the hundreds: 600 + 300 = 900
Add the tens: 20 + 10 = 30
Add the ones: 4 + 5 = 9

Step 3: Combine the place value sums to find the total number:

900 + 30 + 9 = 939

Tall and Wide

Find the sum for each tall and wide addition problem.

4	2	3	6
4	8	3	2
2	5	3	3
3	3	3	1
5	1	5	4
1	1	3	4
+ 7	+ 9	+ 6	+ 10
_____	_____	_____	_____

$3 + 2 + 7 + 7 + 2 + 3 + 3 =$ _____

$6 + 6 + 1 + 3 + 3 + 3 + 4 =$ _____

$10 + 8 + 3 + 5 + 5 + 4 + 6 =$ _____

$8 + 5 + 7 + 6 + 2 + 1 + 3 =$ _____

$4 + 1 + 6 + 9 + 4 + 4 + 2 =$ _____

$7 + 5 + 2 + 3 + 4 + 5 + 2 + 1 + 6 =$ _____

$9 + 0 + 4 + 3 + 3 + 7 + 2 + 3 + 5 =$ _____

BRAIN BOX

The **commutative property** of addition says that you can change the order of addends and still get the same sum. Here's a hint for adding many numbers: reorder the addends to make the math easier!

For example:

$2 + 7 + 5 + 3 + 8$

$2 + 8 + 7 + 3 + 5$

$10 + 10 + 5 = 25$

What's the Difference?

Subtract the numbers to find the **difference**.

```
    48        994        87        867
  - 12      - 542      - 44      - 111
  _____    _____    _____    _____
```

Addition and
subtraction

```
    45        775        399        85
  - 22      - 304      - 144      - 72
  _____    _____    _____    _____
```

```
    97        465        989        876
  - 60      - 323      - 100      - 534
  _____    _____    _____    _____
```

BRAIN BOX

Subtraction is when you take one number away from another number. The answer to a subtraction problem is called the **difference**.

This is one way to subtract multidigit numbers: subtract vertically by place value.

Example: 65 – 21

Step 1:
Subtract the ones.

```
  6 | 5
- 2 | 1
_____
    | 4
```

Step 2:
Subtract the tens.

```
  6 | 5
- 2 | 1
_____
  4 | 4
```

This is another way to subtract multidigit numbers: subtract horizontally by place value.

Example: 978 – 342

Step 1:
Write each number in expanded form.
978 = 900 + 70 + 8
342 = 300 + 40 + 2

Step 2:
Subtract like places.
Subtract the hundreds: 900 – 300 = 600
Subtract the tens: 70 – 40 = 30
Subtract the ones: 8 – 2 = 6

Step 3:
Combine the place value sums to find the difference.
600 + 30 + 6 = 636

Mystery Numbers

Add or **subtract** to find the missing number.

16 minus what mystery number equals 8?

$$16 - \underline{\quad} = 8$$

8

When you subtract me from 24, the difference is 14. What number am I?

My addends are 24 and 35. What is my sum?

21 plus what mystery number equals 36?

35 minus what mystery number equals 20?

41 plus what mystery number equals 56?

My sum is 85. If one of my addends is 63, what is my other addend?

When you add me to 62, the sum is 84. What number am I?

MYSTERY NUMBER

Magic Squares

Fill in the missing numbers so that every row (vertical, horizontal, and diagonal) in the **magic square** adds up to the number in the star.

An addition challenge

4	3	8
9	5	1
2	7	6

⭐ 15

⭐ 27

		6
	9	
12	5	

⭐ 21

	7	
6	11	

BRAIN BOX

In a **magic square**, every row (vertical, horizontal, and diagonal) adds up to the same sum. For example: In this magic square, every row adds up to 18.

9	2	7
4	6	8
5	10	3

Solve the **magic squares**.

13		
6	10	

30

24

	6	11
	8	

16		2	13
			8
	6	7	
4	15		1

34

38

14	9		2
	12		
4			16
17		10	5

An addition challenge

Time to Regroup

Regroup to find the **sum**. Show your work.

Regrouping
in addition

```
  1
  29            65           37
+ 12          + 17         + 28
 ————         ————         ————
  41
```

```
  456          387          546
+ 174        + 264        + 198
 ————         ————         ————
```

```
  308          765          824
+ 199        +  77        + 119
 ————         ————         ————
```

```
  287          196          624
+ 166        + 475        + 299
```

```
  361          698          179
+ 345        + 228        +  50
```

```
  348          497          162
+ 146        + 166        + 458
```

```
  656          393          829
+ 182        + 157        + 119
```

BRAIN BOX

Sometimes you need to **regroup** when you add three-digit numbers.

Example:
```
  3 8 6
+ 1 8 5
```

Step 1: Add the ones column and move the tens digit of the sum over to the tens column.

```
      1
  3 | 8 | 6
+ 1 | 8 | 5
      |   | 1
```

Step 2: Add the tens column, including the number you moved. If the sum is greater than 9, move the tens digit of the sum over to the hundreds column.

```
  1   1
  3 | 8 | 6
+ 1 | 8 | 5
      7 | 1
```

Step 3: Add the hundreds column, including the number you moved.

```
  1   1
  3 | 8 | 6
+ 1 | 8 | 5
  5 | 7 | 1
```

More Regrouping

Regroup to find the **difference**.
Show your work.

Regrouping in subtraction

```
    3 14
    4̶4̶
  -  16
  ─────
     28
```

```
    65
  - 27
  ────
```

```
    34
  - 15
  ────
```

```
    451
  - 192
  ─────
```

```
    838
  - 269
  ─────
```

```
    546
  - 198
  ─────
```

```
    745
  - 166
  ─────
```

```
    635
  - 287
  ─────
```

```
    751
  - 394
  ─────
```

BRAIN BOX

Sometimes you need to **regroup** when you subtract two-digit numbers.

Example:
```
    4 3
  - 1 7
  ─────
```

Step 1: Can you subtract 7 from 3? No. You have to take one group of 10 from the tens column and add it to the ones column.

```
  3 13
  4̶  3̶
 -1  7
```

Step 2: Now you can subtract the ones column.

```
  3 13
  4̶  3̶
 -1  7
 ─────
      6
```

Step 3: Subtract the tens column, using the new tens digit.

```
  3 13
  4̶  3̶
 -1  7
 ─────
  2   6
```

Regroup to find the difference.
Show your work.

Regrouping in subtraction

```
  361          658          679
- 245        - 278        -  80
```

```
  468          817          762
- 179        - 396        - 438
```

```
  656          663          823
- 183        - 190        - 157
```

BRAIN BOX

Sometimes you need to **regroup** when you subtract three-digit numbers.

Example:
```
  6 4 5
- 1 7 8
```

Step 1: Regroup one 10 from the tens column to the ones column in order to subtract the ones.

```
    3 15
  6 4 5
- 1 7 8
      7
```

Step 2: Regroup one 100 from the hundreds column to the tens column in order to subtract the tens.

```
  5 13 15
  6  4  5
- 1  7  8
     6  7
```

Step 3: Subtract the hundreds column using the new hundreds digit.

```
  5 13 15
  6  4  5
- 1  7  8
  4  6  7
```

What About Zeros?

Regroup to find the **difference**. Show your work.

Regrouping in subtraction with zeros

$$
\begin{array}{r}
\overset{9}{\cancel{8}}\;\overset{}{\cancel{10}}\;\overset{}{11} \\
\cancel{901} \\
-\quad 65 \\
\hline
836
\end{array}
$$

$$
\begin{array}{r}
503 \\
-\;\;15 \\
\hline
\end{array}
$$

$$
\begin{array}{r}
802 \\
-\;\;75 \\
\hline
\end{array}
$$

$$
\begin{array}{r}
304 \\
-\;\;77 \\
\hline
\end{array}
$$

$$
\begin{array}{r}
704 \\
-\;168 \\
\hline
\end{array}
$$

$$
\begin{array}{r}
601 \\
-\;\;44 \\
\hline
\end{array}
$$

$$
\begin{array}{r}
705 \\
-\;\;48 \\
\hline
\end{array}
$$

$$
\begin{array}{r}
903 \\
-\;176 \\
\hline
\end{array}
$$

$$
\begin{array}{r}
404 \\
-\;\;66 \\
\hline
\end{array}
$$

BRAIN BOX

In some subtraction problems, you have to **regroup across a zero**.

Example:	4 0 5
	− 3 8

Step 1: To subtract the 8 from the 5 in the ones column, you would ordinarily regroup using the tens column. But since there are no tens, you need to regroup using the hundreds column first. Take one hundred from the hundreds column by crossing out the 4, and write a 10 above the tens column (10 tens = 100).

Step 2: Now you have 10 in the tens column. You can regroup by taking 1 ten from the tens column and adding 10 ones to the ones column. Subtract.

$$
\begin{array}{r}
\overset{3}{\cancel{4}}\;\overset{10}{0}\;5 \\
-\;\;3\;8 \\
\hline
\end{array}
$$

$$
\begin{array}{r}
\overset{}{3}\;\overset{9}{\cancel{10}}\;\overset{15}{} \\
\cancel{4}\;\cancel{0}\;5 \\
-\;\;3\;8 \\
\hline
3\;6\;7
\end{array}
$$

Double Zero

Regroup to find the **difference**. Show your work.

Regrouping in subtraction with zeros

$$
\begin{array}{r}
\overset{9}{\cancel{6}}\,\overset{10}{\cancel{10}}\,10 \\
\cancel{700} \\
-\ 531 \\
\hline
169
\end{array}
$$

$$
\begin{array}{r}
900 \\
-\ 87 \\
\hline
\end{array}
$$

$$
\begin{array}{r}
400 \\
-\ 33 \\
\hline
\end{array}
$$

$$
\begin{array}{r}
300 \\
-\ 168 \\
\hline
\end{array}
$$

$$
\begin{array}{r}
800 \\
-\ 245 \\
\hline
\end{array}
$$

$$
\begin{array}{r}
601 \\
-\ 374 \\
\hline
\end{array}
$$

$$
\begin{array}{r}
200 \\
-\ 36 \\
\hline
\end{array}
$$

$$
\begin{array}{r}
900 \\
-\ 132 \\
\hline
\end{array}
$$

$$
\begin{array}{r}
500 \\
-\ 57 \\
\hline
\end{array}
$$

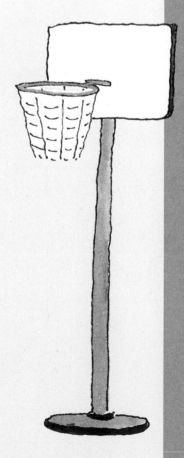

Missing Signs

These equations are missing the **plus** and **minus** signs. In each box, write the sign that makes the equation correct.

Addition or subtraction

9 ☐ 11 = 20

11 ☐ 5 = 6

3 ☐ 6 = 9

125 ☐ 75 = 50

37 ☐ 2 = 35

68 ☐ 12 = 80

12 ☐ 12 ☐ 24 = 0

150 ☐ 100 ☐ 14 = 64

22 ☐ 12 ☐ 11 = 21

21 ☐ 33 ☐ 3 = 57

33 ☐ 11 ☐ 10 = 34

47 ☐ 15 ☐ 3 = 29

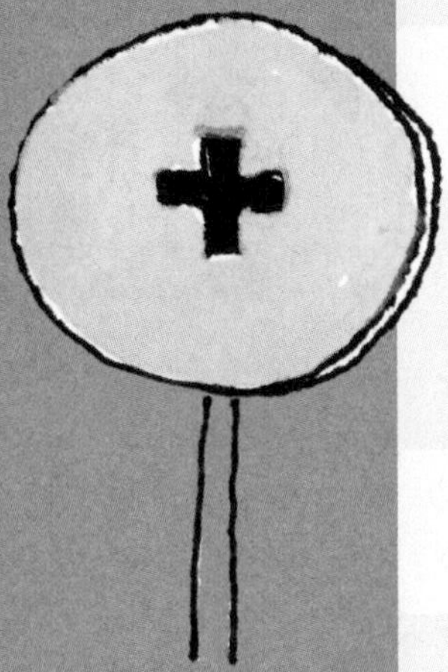

Sum Time

Find the **sum** for each addition problem.
You may need to regroup.

Addition practice

$$277 + 111$$

$$254 + 269$$

$$833 + 144$$

$$666 + 224$$

$$156 + 222$$

$$752 + 60$$

$$378 + 167$$

$$844 + 235$$

$$161 + 428$$

$$672 + 153$$

$$500 + 266$$

$$708 + 188$$

$$338 + 116$$

$$453 + 71$$

$$330 + 169$$

Take It Away

Find the **difference** for each subtraction problem.
You may need to regroup.

Subtraction
practice

$$756 - 111$$

$$330 - 119$$

$$807 - 335$$

$$669 - 226$$

$$763 - 152$$

$$842 - 60$$

$$752 - 116$$

$$500 - 176$$

$$864 - 424$$

$$876 - 234$$

$$703 - 162$$

$$847 - 146$$

$$900 - 188$$

$$756 - 71$$

$$752 - 711$$

MULTIPLICATION AND DIVISION

What time is it? It's times tables time! Let's practice multiplying numbers 0 through 12 and then use what we know about multiplication to do some division.

PARENTS Third graders are ready for multiplication and to understand how it builds on addition. Fill out a multiplication chart with your child so that you can explore the relationships between the numbers. Talk about the patterns you see together.

Multiplying by One

Find the **product**.

$$\begin{array}{r} 1 \\ \times\ 6 \\ \hline 6 \end{array} \qquad \begin{array}{r} 7 \\ \times\ 1 \\ \hline \end{array} \qquad \begin{array}{r} 1 \\ \times\ 5 \\ \hline \end{array} \qquad \begin{array}{r} 8 \\ \times\ 1 \\ \hline \end{array}$$

$$\begin{array}{r} 1 \\ \times\ 0 \\ \hline \end{array} \qquad \begin{array}{r} 1 \\ \times\ 3 \\ \hline \end{array} \qquad \begin{array}{r} 2 \\ \times\ 1 \\ \hline \end{array} \qquad \begin{array}{r} 1 \\ \times\ 1 \\ \hline \end{array}$$

$$\begin{array}{r} 4 \\ \times\ 1 \\ \hline \end{array} \qquad \begin{array}{r} 1 \\ \times\ 4 \\ \hline \end{array} \qquad \begin{array}{r} 9 \\ \times\ 1 \\ \hline \end{array} \qquad \begin{array}{r} 1 \\ \times\ 2 \\ \hline \end{array}$$

Multiplication

> **QUICK FACT:**
> When you multiply any number by 1, the product is the other number.

10 × 1 = ___   6 × 1 = ___   5 × 1 = ___   7 × 1 = ___

Fill in the multiplication chart.

×	1	2	3	4	5	6	7	8	9	10
1	1									

BRAIN BOX

Multiplication is the same as repeated addition. The **product** is the answer when two or more numbers are multiplied.

Multiplying by Two

Find the **product.**

2 × 1	3 × 2	2 × 6	7 × 2
2 × 5	2 × 4	5 × 2	2 × 8
10 × 2	2 × 2	2 × 9	6 × 2

Multiplication

QUICK FACT: When you multiply any number by 0, the product is 0.

2 × 3 = ___   4 × 2 = ___   9 × 2 = ___   2 × 0 = ___

Fill in the multiplication chart.

×	1	2	3	4	5	6	7	8	9	10
2										

Multiplying by Three

Find the **product.**

3 × 1	3 × 7	0 × 3	3 × 4
10 × 3	3 × 3	3 × 6	2 × 3
9 × 3	3 × 5	7 × 3	5 × 3

4 × 3 = ___   3 × 8 = ___   6 × 3 = ___   3 × 10 = __

Fill in the multiplication chart.

×	1	2	3	4	5	6	7	8	9	10
3										

BRAIN BOX

When we see a multiplication problem like 3 x 7, we read it as "three **times** seven." But you can also say "three **groups of** seven."

3 groups of 7 can look like this

or like this: 7 + 7 + 7.

Multiplying by Four

Find the **product**.

Multiplication

$$\begin{array}{r} 2 \\ \times\ 4 \\ \hline \end{array} \qquad \begin{array}{r} 8 \\ \times\ 4 \\ \hline \end{array} \qquad \begin{array}{r} 4 \\ \times\ 6 \\ \hline \end{array} \qquad \begin{array}{r} 3 \\ \times\ 4 \\ \hline \end{array}$$

$$\begin{array}{r} 4 \\ \times\ 5 \\ \hline \end{array} \qquad \begin{array}{r} 10 \\ \times\ 4 \\ \hline \end{array}$$

$$\begin{array}{r} 9 \\ \times\ 4 \\ \hline \end{array} \qquad \begin{array}{r} 4 \\ \times\ 1 \\ \hline \end{array}$$

$$\begin{array}{r} 7 \\ \times\ 4 \\ \hline \end{array} \qquad \begin{array}{r} 4 \\ \times\ 2 \\ \hline \end{array} \qquad \begin{array}{r} 4 \\ \times\ 9 \\ \hline \end{array} \qquad \begin{array}{r} 6 \\ \times\ 4 \\ \hline \end{array}$$

$4 \times 3 =$ ___ $4 \times 4 =$ ___

$5 \times 4 =$ ___ $0 \times 4 =$ ___

Fill in the multiplication chart.

✕	1	2	3	4	5	6	7	8	9	10
4										

Multiplying by Five

Find the **product**.

5 × 4	5 × 5	2 × 5	7 × 5
9 × 5	0 × 5	10 × 5	5 × 8
1 × 5	5 × 2	5 × 9	6 × 5

3 × 5 = ___   5 × 4 = ___   5 × 8 = ___   5 × 3 = ___

Fill in the multiplication chart.

×	1	2	3	4	5	6	7	8	9	10
5										

Multiplying by Six

Find the **product.**

2 × 6	6 × 0	5 × 6	7 × 6
3 × 6	6 × 4	6 × 2	6 × 8
9 × 6	6 × 6	6 × 5	6 × 3

Multiplication

10 × 6 = __

6 × 4 = __

9 × 6 = __

6 × 1 = __

Fill in the multiplication chart.

✕	1	2	3	4	5	6	7	8	9	10
6										

Multiplying by Seven

Find the **product**.

7 × 6	1 × 7	5 × 7	7 × 7
3 × 7	7 × 4	8 × 7	0 × 7
7 × 1	9 × 7	7 × 2	10 × 7

5 × 7 = ___   7 × 4 = ___   9 × 7 = ___   8 × 7 = ___

Fill in the multiplication chart.

×	1	2	3	4	5	6	7	8	9	10
7										

Multiplying by Eight

Find the **product.**

Multiplication

7 × 8	8 × 6	8 × 4	10 × 8
8 × 5	8 × 7	0 × 8	3 × 8
9 × 8	2 × 8	8 × 8	8 × 2

8 × 6 = ___	8 × 5 = ___	10 × 8 = ___	8 × 7 = ___

Fill in the multiplication chart.

×	1	2	3	4	5	6	7	8	9	10
8										

Multiplying by Nine

Find the **product.**

$\begin{array}{r} 1 \\ \times\ 9 \\ \hline \end{array}$	$\begin{array}{r} 9 \\ \times\ 7 \\ \hline \end{array}$	$\begin{array}{r} 5 \\ \times\ 9 \\ \hline \end{array}$	$\begin{array}{r} 9 \\ \times\ 9 \\ \hline \end{array}$
$\begin{array}{r} 3 \\ \times\ 9 \\ \hline \end{array}$	$\begin{array}{r} 6 \\ \times\ 9 \\ \hline \end{array}$	$\begin{array}{r} 9 \\ \times\ 2 \\ \hline \end{array}$	$\begin{array}{r} 9 \\ \times\ 0 \\ \hline \end{array}$
$\begin{array}{r} 9 \\ \times\ 6 \\ \hline \end{array}$	$\begin{array}{r} 4 \\ \times\ 9 \\ \hline \end{array}$	$\begin{array}{r} 9 \\ \times\ 8 \\ \hline \end{array}$	$\begin{array}{r} 10 \\ \times\ 9 \\ \hline \end{array}$

5 × 9 = ___   9 × 8 = ___   9 × 7 = ___   4 × 9 = ___

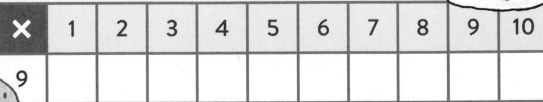

Fill in the multiplication chart.

×	1	2	3	4	5	6	7	8	9	10
9										

Helping Hands

Do you have trouble multiplying by 9? Here's an easy trick to help you.

Multiplying by nine

- Hold up both of your hands with your fingers spread apart.

- Let's use 9 × 3 as an example.
  Bend down your third finger from the left.
  You'll see 2 fingers to the left of your bent finger and 7 fingers to the right of your bent finger.
  The answer to 9 × 3 is 27.

- Try it again to find the answer to 9 × 6.
  Bend down your sixth finger from the left.
  You'll see 5 fingers to the left of your bent finger and 4 fingers to the right of your bent finger.
  The answer to 9 × 6 is 54.

- This works for 9 × 1 through 9 × 10.
  Isn't it a handy trick?

Use the trick you just learned to solve each problem.

9 × 4 = _____   9 × 3 = _____

9 × 8 = _____   9 × 9 = _____

9 × 6 = _____   9 × 1 = _____

9 × 2 = _____   9 × 7 = _____

9 × 5 = _____   9 × 10 = _____

Multiplying by Ten

Find the **product**.

Multiplication

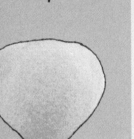

10 × 1	4 × 10	10 × 8
10 × 7	10 × 9	6 × 10
5 × 10	10 × 10	10 × 4

10 × 3 = ____   2 × 10 = ____

10 × 7 = ____

Fill in the multiplication chart.

×	1	2	3	4	5	6	7	8	9	10
10										

BRAIN BOX

When you multiply by 10, move the digit in the ones place to the tens place and put a zero in the ones place.

Times Table to Twelve

Find the **product.**

1 × 1	2 × 2	3 × 3	4 × 4
5 × 5	6 × 6	7 × 7	8 × 8
9 × 9	10 × 10	11 × 11	12 × 12

Multiplication

QUICK FACT:
When you multiply a number by itself, it is called a **square number.**

Fill in the multiplication charts.

×	1	2	3	4	5	6	7	8	9	10
11										

×	1	2	3	4	5	6	7	8	9	10
12										

Practice Problems

Find the **products** of each multiplication problem.

Commutative property

$$\begin{array}{r} 9 \\ \times\ 4 \\ \hline 36 \end{array}$$ $$\begin{array}{r} 4 \\ \times\ 9 \\ \hline 36 \end{array}$$

$$\begin{array}{r} 8 \\ \times\ 3 \\ \hline \end{array}$$ $$\begin{array}{r} 3 \\ \times\ 8 \\ \hline \end{array}$$

$$\begin{array}{r} 7 \\ \times\ 8 \\ \hline \end{array}$$ $$\begin{array}{r} 8 \\ \times\ 7 \\ \hline \end{array}$$

$$\begin{array}{r} 2 \\ \times\ 7 \\ \hline \end{array}$$ $$\begin{array}{r} 7 \\ \times\ 2 \\ \hline \end{array}$$

$$\begin{array}{r} 5 \\ \times\ 4 \\ \hline \end{array}$$ $$\begin{array}{r} 4 \\ \times\ 5 \\ \hline \end{array}$$

$$\begin{array}{r} 6 \\ \times\ 5 \\ \hline \end{array}$$ $$\begin{array}{r} 5 \\ \times\ 6 \\ \hline \end{array}$$

BRAIN BOX

The product of two or more numbers will always be the same, no matter in which order you multiply them. This is called the **commutative property of multiplication**. For example: 9 × 3 = 27 and 3 × 9 = 27

Using the rule in the Brain Box, try this problem.

$$\begin{array}{r} 998 \\ \times\ 730 \\ \hline 728{,}540 \end{array}$$ $$\begin{array}{r} 730 \\ \times\ 998 \\ \hline \end{array}$$

Hop, Skip, and Jump

In each row, **skip count** by the number shown in the star. You can use multiplication facts to help.

Skip counting for multiplication

| 4 | 8 | 12 | 16 | 20 | 24 | 28 | 32 | 36 | 40 |

| 5 | _ | _ | _ | 30 | _ | _ | _ | _ | 50 |

| 6 | _ | 24 | _ | _ | 48 | _ | 60 |

| _ | 21 | _ | 35 | _ | 56 | _ | _ |

| 8 | _ | _ | 40 | _ | 64 | _ | 80 |

BRAIN BOX

Skip counting is when you count forward (or backward) by a number other than one. When we skip count by three it looks like this: 3, 6, 9, 12, 15, 18, 21, 24 . . .

Missing Numbers

Complete each equation by writing the missing number in the box.

Multiplication challenge

$2 \times \boxed{4} = 8$

$\boxed{} \times 7 = 42$

$\boxed{} \times 8 = 64$

$5 \times 7 = \boxed{}$

$\boxed{} \times 9 = 36$

$\boxed{} \times 8 = 48$

$3 \times 7 = \boxed{}$

$9 \times \boxed{} = 0$

$4 \times 7 = \boxed{}$

$1 \times 10 = \boxed{}$

$4 \times 8 = \boxed{}$

$2 \times \boxed{} = 12$

$7 \times \boxed{} = 49$

$\boxed{} \times 9 = 72$

$\boxed{} \times 3 = 18$

$\boxed{} \times 2 = 10$

$\boxed{} \times 9 = 54$

$9 \times \boxed{} = 27$

The Product Finder

Complete the **multiplication table** by filling in the missing numbers.

Addition and multiplication

×	0	1	2	3	4	5	6	7	8	9	10	11	12
0	0												
1		1											
2			4										
3				9		15						33	
4													48
5	0							35					
6										54			
7							42						
8													
9													108
10											100		
11													
12													144

BRAIN BOX

Take a look. One half of the multiplication table is a mirror image of the other. Instead of memorizing 2 × 5 and *also* 5 × 2, memorize, or better yet, understand that 2 and 5 multiplied equal 10.

×	1	2	3	4	5	6	7	8	9	10
1	1	2	3	4	5	6	7	8	9	10
2	2	4	6	8	10	12	14	16	18	20
3	3	6	9	12	15	16	21	24	27	30
4	4	8	12	16	20	24	28	32	36	40
5	5	10	15	20	25	30	35	40	45	50
6	6	12	18	24	30	36	42	48	54	60
7	7	14	21	28	35	42	49	56	63	70
8	8	16	24	32	40	48	56	64	72	80
9	9	18	27	36	45	54	63	72	82	90
10	10	20	30	40	50	60	70	80	90	100

The Same!

MULTIPLICATION AND DIVISION

Double Digit!

Find the **product**.

$$
\begin{array}{r}
14 \\
\times\ 2 \\
\hline
28
\end{array}
\qquad
\begin{array}{r}
62 \\
\times\ 3 \\
\hline
\end{array}
\qquad
\begin{array}{r}
31 \\
\times\ 5 \\
\hline
\end{array}
\qquad
\begin{array}{r}
52 \\
\times\ 4 \\
\hline
\end{array}
$$

Two-digit multiplication

$$
\begin{array}{r}
12 \\
\times\ 7 \\
\hline
\end{array}
\qquad
\begin{array}{r}
80 \\
\times\ 9 \\
\hline
\end{array}
\qquad
\begin{array}{r}
61 \\
\times\ 8 \\
\hline
\end{array}
\qquad
\begin{array}{r}
73 \\
\times\ 3 \\
\hline
\end{array}
$$

$$
\begin{array}{r}
98 \\
\times\ 1 \\
\hline
\end{array}
\qquad
\begin{array}{r}
44 \\
\times\ 2 \\
\hline
\end{array}
\qquad
\begin{array}{r}
52 \\
\times\ 3 \\
\hline
\end{array}
\qquad
\begin{array}{r}
60 \\
\times\ 9 \\
\hline
\end{array}
$$

1 × 98 = ___   2 × 44 = ___   3 × 52 = ___   9 × 60 = ___

BRAIN BOX

This is how to multiply 2-digit numbers.

Example:
$$
\begin{array}{r}
4\ 3 \\
\times\ 2 \\
\hline
\end{array}
$$

Step 1: Multiply the digits in the ones column. Write the product below the ones.

$$
\begin{array}{r}
4\ 3 \\
\times\ 2 \\
\hline
6
\end{array}
$$

Step 2: Multiply the tens digit by 2. Write the product under the tens column.

$$
\begin{array}{r}
4\ 3 \\
\times\ 2 \\
\hline
8\ 6
\end{array}
$$

Regroup It!

Find the **product.** Show your work.

$$\begin{array}{r} 69 \\ \times\ 3 \\ \hline \end{array}$$

$$\begin{array}{r} 36 \\ \times\ 8 \\ \hline \end{array}$$

$$\begin{array}{r} 78 \\ \times\ 4 \\ \hline \end{array}$$

$$\begin{array}{r} 45 \\ \times\ 5 \\ \hline \end{array}$$

$$\begin{array}{r} 82 \\ \times\ 7 \\ \hline \end{array}$$

$$\begin{array}{r} 26 \\ \times\ 3 \\ \hline \end{array}$$

$$\begin{array}{r} 52 \\ \times\ 8 \\ \hline \end{array}$$

$$\begin{array}{r} 66 \\ \times\ 9 \\ \hline \end{array}$$

$$\begin{array}{r} 85 \\ \times\ 7 \\ \hline \end{array}$$

6 × 94 = _____

5 × 37 = _____

8 × 48 = _____

BRAIN BOX

Another way to multiply is by using the **partial products** strategy.

Example: 18 × 5 = _____

10 × 5 = 50
8 × 5 = 40
50 + 40 = 90

Step 1: Multiply by place value. Start with the tens. (The 1 in 18 stands for 10—multiply that by 5.)

10 × 5 = 50

Step 2: Multiply the ones. (The 8 in 18 stands for 8 ones—multiply that by 5.)

8 × 5 = 40

Step 3: Add the partial products from steps 1 and 2 to find the product:

50 + 40 = 90

18 × 5 = 90

Finding Quotients

Find the **quotient.**

Division terms and basic rules

$16 \div 2 = \boxed{8}$ $2\overline{)16}$ with $\boxed{8}$ on top

Psst—here's a hint: Find the answer by using your multiplication facts.

$2 \times \boxed{?} = 16$

The answer is $\boxed{8}$.

$9 \div 3 = \boxed{}$ $3\overline{)9}$ with $\boxed{}$ on top

$12 \div 4 = \boxed{}$ $4\overline{)12}$ with $\boxed{}$ on top

$6 \div 2 = \boxed{}$ $2\overline{)6}$ with $\boxed{}$ on top

BRAIN BOX

Division is the process of taking one number and splitting, or dividing, it into equal groups. The number being divided is the **dividend**. The number we divide by is the **divisor**. The answer to a division problem is called the **quotient**.

Example: 5 ← quotient
divisor → 3 $\overline{)15}$ ← dividend

The Missing Divisors

Find the **quotient.**

☐ $2\overline{)\,8}$ ☐ $3\overline{)\,6}$ ☐ $2\overline{)\,12}$ ☐ $3\overline{)\,15}$

A division challenge

☐ $5\overline{)\,10}$ ☐ $2\overline{)\,20}$ ☐ $8\overline{)\,16}$ ☐ $2\overline{)\,22}$

QUICK FACT: Any number except zero divided by itself is always 1.

☐ $8\overline{)\,32}$ ☐ $7\overline{)\,21}$ ☐ $6\overline{)\,24}$ ☐ $6\overline{)\,36}$

☐ $5\overline{)\,40}$ ☐ $2\overline{)\,14}$ ☐ $4\overline{)\,8}$ ☐ $1\overline{)\,9}$

3 ÷ 3 = _____   18 ÷ 2 = _____

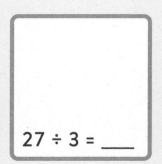

27 ÷ 3 = _____   30 ÷ 3 = _____

Math Matters

Find the **quotient**.

Henry is building bird feeders for his neighbors. He bought 18 feet of wood. If each bird feeder requires 2 feet, how many bird feeders can he build?

18 ÷ 2 = ▢

Luca baked a loaf of bread 12 inches long. He needs to cut it into 3 equal pieces. How many inches long will each piece be?

12 ÷ ▢ = ▢

The architect designed the library to have 48 windows. If there is an equal number of windows on the 4 walls, and windows are divided equally among its 4 walls, how many windows are on each wall?

48 ÷ ▢ = ▢

The student art show has a total of 12 paintings. If the paintings are hung on 2 walls, how many will be on each wall? Draw the groups and write the equation.

▢ ÷ ▢ = ▢

If the paintings are hung on 3 walls, how many will be hung on each wall? Draw the groups and write the equation.

▢ ÷ ▢ = ▢

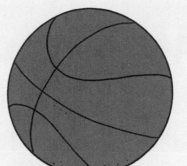

Our basketball team scored 20 points in the first quarter! Each team member on the court scored 4 points. How many team members were on the court?

☐ ÷ ☐ = ☐

The scientist has 30 test tubes in her laboratory. Each tray holds 5 test tubes. How many trays did she use?

☐ ÷ ☐ = ☐

The building is 88 feet high. Each floor is 11 feet. How many floors are there?

☐ ÷ ☐ = ☐

Third grade collected 56 books during their book drive. They stored 8 books in each box. How many boxes were there?

☐ ÷ ☐ = ☐

Our class has a community garden. If we planted 18 lettuce seeds in 3 rows, how many seeds did we plant in each row?

☐ ÷ ☐ = ☐

Math House

Only **fact families** live in this house. Write the four facts for the fact family in each room of the house.

MULTIPLICATION AND DIVISION

Fact families

20
5
4

$4 \times 5 = 20$
$5 \times 4 = 20$
$20 \div 4 = 5$
$20 \div 5 = 4$

12
3
4

32
8
4

35
7
5

28
7
4

45
9
5

BRAIN BOX

A multiplication and division **fact family** is a set of related multiplication and division equations that use the same numbers. Each fact family has two multiplication equations and two division equations using the same three numbers.

For example, the fact family for **2, 7,** and **14** is:

$2 \times 7 = 14$ $7 \times 2 = 14$
$14 \div 2 = 7$ $14 \div 7 = 2$

Brain Quest Grade 3 Workbook

Math Building

Only **fact families** live in this building.
Write down the four facts for the fact family
in each room of the building.

Fact families

9		6	
2		5	
18		30	

6		9	
2		8	
12		72	

48		7	
6		8	
8		56	

40		9	
5		7	
8		63	

Watch the Signs!

Complete each equation with a **multiplication** or **division** sign.

Multiplication and division signs

$8 \div 8 = 1$

$8 \boxed{} 8 = 64$ $18 \boxed{} 9 = 2$ $6 \boxed{} 5 = 30$

$7 \boxed{} 9 = 63$ $7 \boxed{} 2 = 14$ $64 \boxed{} 8 = 8$

$32 \boxed{} 4 = 8$ $27 \boxed{} 3 = 9$ $8 \boxed{} 2 = 4$

$9 \boxed{} 5 = 45$ $6 \boxed{} 8 = 48$ $12 \boxed{} 3 = 4$

$6 \boxed{} 3 = 2$ $9 \boxed{} 3 = 3$ $3 \boxed{} 7 = 21$

$49 \boxed{} 7 = 7$

$2 \boxed{} 4 = 8$

$56 \boxed{} 7 = 8$

Practice!

Multiply or **divide**.

Multiplication and division

$$
\begin{array}{r}
9 \\
\times\ 3 \\
\hline
\end{array}
$$

$$
\begin{array}{r}
4 \\
\times\ 9 \\
\hline
\end{array}
$$

$3\overline{)21}$

$$
\begin{array}{r}
7 \\
\times\ 4 \\
\hline
\end{array}
$$

$6\overline{)24}$

$8\overline{)32}$

$$
\begin{array}{r}
7 \\
\times\ 7 \\
\hline
\end{array}
$$

$$
\begin{array}{r}
9 \\
\times\ 7 \\
\hline
\end{array}
$$

$$
\begin{array}{r}
9 \\
\times\ 6 \\
\hline
\end{array}
$$

$7\overline{)28}$

$$
\begin{array}{r}
3 \\
\times\ 8 \\
\hline
\end{array}
$$

$9\overline{)45}$

$$
\begin{array}{r}
4 \\
\times\ 9 \\
\hline
\end{array}
$$

$$
\begin{array}{r}
3 \\
\times\ 9 \\
\hline
\end{array}
$$

$$
\begin{array}{r}
6 \\
\times\ 7 \\
\hline
\end{array}
$$

$4\overline{)12}$

$3 \times 65 = \underline{\quad}$

$5 \times 5 = \underline{\quad}$

$4 \times 4 = \underline{\quad}$

$81 \div 9 = \underline{\quad}$

A Bike Ride

A group of friends is going on a bike ride. Use what you know about **multiplication** and **division** to answer the word problems.

Multiplication and division

The group includes 10 kids: 6 riding bicycles and 4 riding tricycles. How many wheels are there in total?

If the group passes 3 houses per minute, how many houses will they pass if they bike for 9 minutes?

The group stops for a snack. Simone brought a bag of popcorn with 30 pieces in it. If she gives everyone the same amount, how many pieces can each person have?

Deandre can travel the length of one block in 30 seconds. How many seconds would it take him to travel the length of the 4 blocks?

BONUS! How many *minutes* would it take Deandre to travel the length of the block 4 times?

FRACTIONS AND DECIMALS

Sharing is caring! When you understand how fractions work, you can share better—and more fairly—with friends.

PARENTS In third grade, children begin focusing on fractions and decimals, laying the foundation for future math. Fractions and decimals are not whole numbers—using concrete images like pictures and fraction models help children understand these complex ideas.

PLACE A
STICKER
HERE

For additional resources, visit www.BrainQuest.com/grade3

Hello Fractions!

Answer the questions about **fractions**.

Write your answers in the colored boxes.

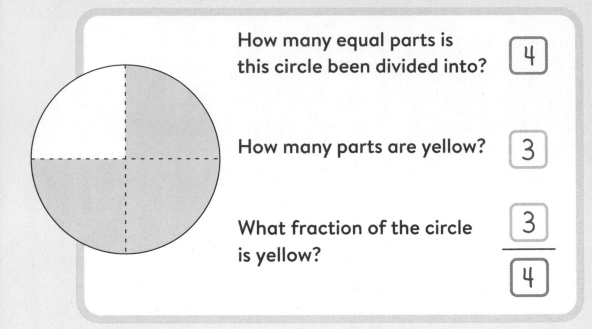

How many equal parts is this circle been divided into? `4`

How many parts are yellow? `3`

What fraction of the circle is yellow? $\dfrac{3}{4}$

How many parts has this rectangle been divided into? ☐

How many parts have been colored yellow? ☐

What fraction of the rectangle has been colored yellow? $\dfrac{\Box}{\Box}$

BRAIN BOX

A **fraction** represents one or more parts of a whole.

A fraction is made up of two numbers. The top number is called the **numerator**. The bottom number is called the **denominator**.

Answer the questions about **fractions.**

Fraction basics

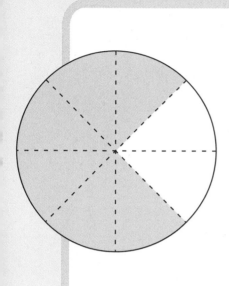

How many parts has this circle been divided into?

How many parts have been colored yellow?

What fraction of the circle has been colored yellow?

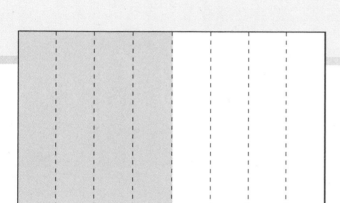

How many parts has this rectangle been divided into?

How many parts have been colored yellow?

What fraction of the rectangle has been colored yellow?

BRAIN BOX

The **numerator** tells us how many parts of the whole we are counting. The **denominator** tells us the total number of parts in the whole.

Example: $\dfrac{3}{4}$ ← numerator
← denominator

This fraction tells us there are three out of four parts. This fraction is **three-fourths.**

Fraction Action

What **fractions** of these shapes have been colored?
Write the correct fractions under the shapes.

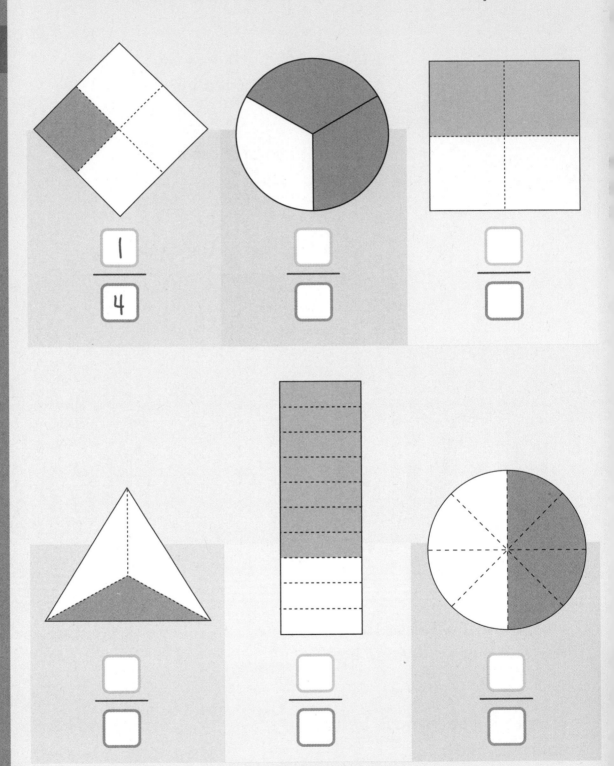

Color the shapes.

Fraction basics

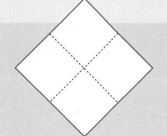

Color $\frac{3}{4}$ of this diamond red

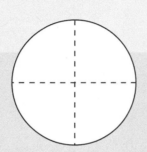

Color $\frac{1}{2}$ of this rectangle orange.

Color $\frac{1}{4}$ of this square blue.

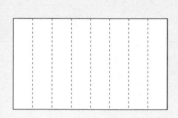

Color $\frac{2}{8}$ of this rectangle green.

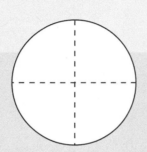

Color $\frac{2}{4}$ of this circle purple.

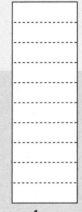

Color $\frac{4}{10}$ of this rectangle pink.

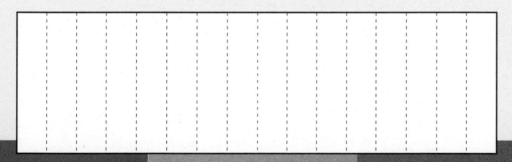

Color $\frac{1}{16}$ of this rectangle red.

Color $\frac{2}{16}$ of this rectangle blue.

Color $\frac{4}{16}$ of this rectangle purple.

Color $\frac{3}{16}$ of this rectangle orange.

Color $\frac{5}{16}$ of this rectangle green.

What fraction of the rectangle is left white?

The Dog Show

Use the picture to answer the questions.

Identifying fractions

What fraction of the dogs are spotted? $\dfrac{3}{10}$

What fraction of the dogs are brown? $\dfrac{}{}$

What fraction of the dogs are black? $\dfrac{}{}$

What fraction of the dogs have a bone? $\dfrac{}{}$

What fraction of the dogs are standing? $\dfrac{}{}$

Be Fair!

Answer the following **fraction** problems. Write the fraction that names one group.

Mr. Johnson has 9 dollar bills. He wants to give an equal number of dollars to each of his 3 sons. Divide the dollars into 3 equal groups by circling each group.

Fractions

Ms. Mathias has 10 cookies to hand out to her students. She has 5 children in her class. Divide the cookies evenly so that each student receives the same amount of cookies.

Tammy has 16 strawberries. She wants to divide them evenly between herself and her 3 friends. Divide the strawberries into 4 equal parts by circling each part.

Rosie's Restaurant

Read each **fraction** problem. Write the equation in the box. Then write your answer on the line.

Dividing whole numbers into fractions

Rosie's Restaurant has 20 tables. $\frac{1}{4}$ of the tables are empty. How many of the tables are empty?

$20 \div 4 = 5$ $\frac{1}{4}$ of 20 = __5__

There are 6 diners at one of the tables. $\frac{1}{2}$ of those 6 diners have ordered chicken. How many have ordered chicken?

÷   = $\frac{1}{2}$ of 6 = ____

10 diners are sitting at a corner table. $\frac{1}{5}$ of them have ordered peach pie. How many have ordered peach pie?

÷   = $\frac{1}{5}$ of 10 = ____

There is a group of 8 people waiting to be seated. $\frac{1}{2}$ of those people are men. How many in that group are men?

÷   = $\frac{1}{2}$ of 8 = ____

Solve the **fraction** problems.

At a table with 4 diners, $\frac{1}{2}$ have ordered baked potatoes. How many have ordered baked potatoes?

÷	=

$\frac{1}{2}$ of 4 = ____

Dividing whole numbers into fractions

There are 15 different desserts on the menu. $\frac{1}{3}$ of them are cakes. How many of the desserts are cakes?

÷	=

$\frac{1}{3}$ of 15 = ____

There are 16 burgers on the grill. $\frac{1}{2}$ of them have cheese on them. How many are cheeseburgers?

÷	=

$\frac{1}{2}$ of 16 = ____

At a table in the back there are 15 diners. $\frac{1}{5}$ of them have ordered spare ribs. How many have ordered spare ribs?

÷	=

$\frac{1}{5}$ of 15 = ____

At a table near the door, a couple had ordered a large pizza that was cut in 12 slices. They left $\frac{1}{6}$ of it uneaten because they were too full. How many slices didn't they eat?

÷	=

$\frac{1}{6}$ of 12 = ____

Equivalent fractions

Exactly the Same

Color $\frac{1}{2}$ of this rectangle yellow.

Color $\frac{2}{4}$ of this rectangle yellow.

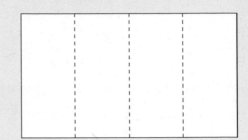

$\frac{1}{2}$ and $\frac{2}{4}$ are **equivalent fractions**—they both equal the same amount.

Write the equivalent fractions for each figure.

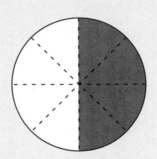

$\frac{4}{8}$

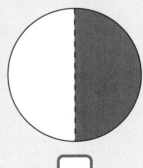

$\frac{\square}{\square}$

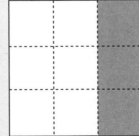

$\frac{3}{9}$

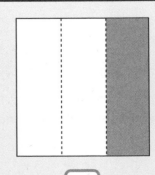

$\frac{\square}{\square}$

Adding Fractions

Add the fractions.

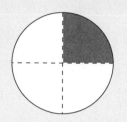 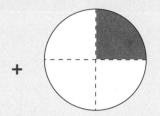 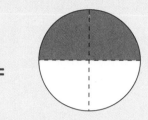

$$\frac{1}{4} \quad + \quad \frac{1}{4} \quad = \quad \frac{\square}{\square}$$

Equivalent fractions

$$\frac{2}{6} \quad + \quad \frac{3}{6} \quad = \quad \frac{\square}{\square}$$

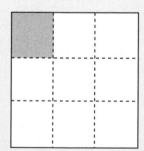 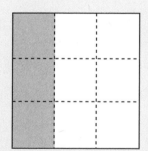 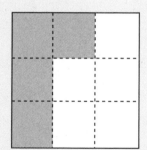

$$\frac{1}{9} \quad + \quad \frac{3}{9} \quad = \quad \frac{\square}{\square}$$

BRAIN BOX

To **add fractions** that have the same denominator, add the numerators. The denominator remains the same.

Adding Fractions

Add the fractions.

Adding
fractions

$\frac{1}{3} + \frac{1}{3} = \frac{2}{3}$

$\frac{1}{5} + \frac{3}{5} = \frac{\boxed{}}{\boxed{}}$

$\frac{1}{4} + \frac{3}{4} = \frac{\boxed{}}{\boxed{}}$

$\frac{2}{4} + \frac{1}{4} = \frac{\boxed{}}{\boxed{}}$

$\frac{8}{10} + \frac{1}{10} = \frac{\boxed{}}{\boxed{}}$

$\frac{3}{6} + \frac{1}{6} = \frac{\boxed{}}{\boxed{}}$

$\frac{8}{12} + \frac{1}{12} = \frac{\boxed{}}{\boxed{}}$

$\frac{3}{8} + \frac{4}{8} = \frac{\boxed{}}{\boxed{}}$

Jared and Derek each ate $\frac{1}{5}$ of a pie. What fraction of the pie was eaten altogether?

Jen poured $\frac{1}{4}$ cup of flour into the cake mix. Her mother poured in another $\frac{1}{4}$ cup. How much flour was in the cake mix?

Subtracting Fractions

Subtract the fractions.

$\dfrac{5}{6} - \dfrac{1}{6} = \dfrac{\boxed{4}}{\boxed{6}}$

$\dfrac{4}{5} - \dfrac{2}{5} = \dfrac{\boxed{}}{\boxed{}}$

$\dfrac{8}{7} - \dfrac{4}{7} = \dfrac{\boxed{}}{\boxed{}}$

$\dfrac{3}{4} - \dfrac{1}{4} = \dfrac{\boxed{}}{\boxed{}}$

$\dfrac{8}{12} - \dfrac{1}{12} = \dfrac{\boxed{}}{\boxed{}}$

$\dfrac{3}{8} - \dfrac{1}{8} = \dfrac{\boxed{}}{\boxed{}}$

$\dfrac{5}{10} - \dfrac{2}{10} = \dfrac{\boxed{}}{\boxed{}}$

$\dfrac{8}{9} - \dfrac{4}{9} = \dfrac{\boxed{}}{\boxed{}}$

Stephen and his brother Mark make up $\dfrac{2}{5}$ of the children in their family. What fraction do the other children in the family make up?

$\dfrac{\boxed{}}{\boxed{}}$

Diana picked $\dfrac{3}{6}$ of the apples from the tree. What fraction of the apples were left for Serena to pick?

$\dfrac{\boxed{}}{\boxed{}}$

BRAIN BOX

To **subtract fractions** that have the same denominators, subtract the numerators. The denominator remains the same.

Bits and Pieces

Write the fractions described by the words.

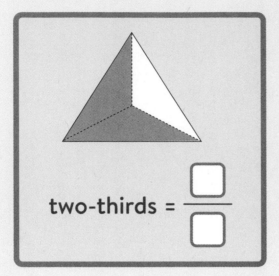

two-thirds = $\frac{\square}{\square}$

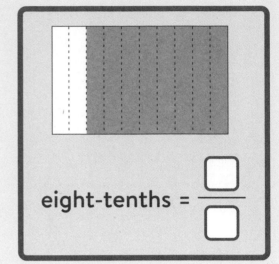

eight-tenths = $\frac{\square}{\square}$

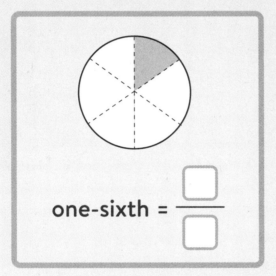

one-sixth = $\frac{\square}{\square}$

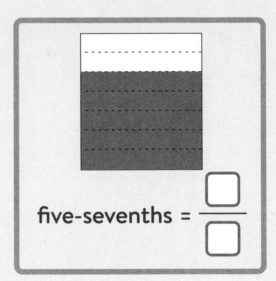

five-sevenths = $\frac{\square}{\square}$

Answer each question. Show your work.

How much is $\frac{1}{3}$ of 21? ___7___

$21 \div 3 = 7$

How much is $\frac{1}{8}$ of 16? ____

How much is $\frac{1}{2}$ of 18? ____

How much is $\frac{1}{10}$ of 20? ____

How much is $\frac{1}{4}$ of 24? ____

Fractions
review

Answer each question.

Jasmine ate $\frac{3}{8}$ of the raisins.

What fraction of
the raisins were left?

Sean ate $\frac{3}{10}$ of the walnuts

Josh ate $\frac{4}{10}$ of the walnuts.

What fraction of
the walnuts were left?

Draw a line from each
fraction in the left column
to the equivalent fraction
in the right column.

What whole number is
equal to $\frac{7}{7} + \frac{7}{7}$? _____

How many sixths equal
one? _____

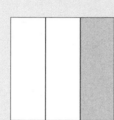

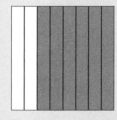

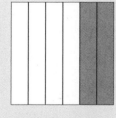
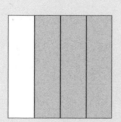

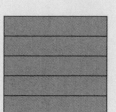
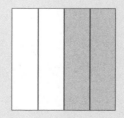

Juanita ate $\frac{1}{2}$ of the
pie at lunch and the
other $\frac{1}{2}$ after school.

What fraction of the
pie did she eat?

BRAIN BOX

When a fraction has the same
numerator and denominator, the
fraction equals 1.

What's the Point?

What fraction of each shape is shaded?
Write the fraction and its **decimal** equivalent.

Converting to decimals

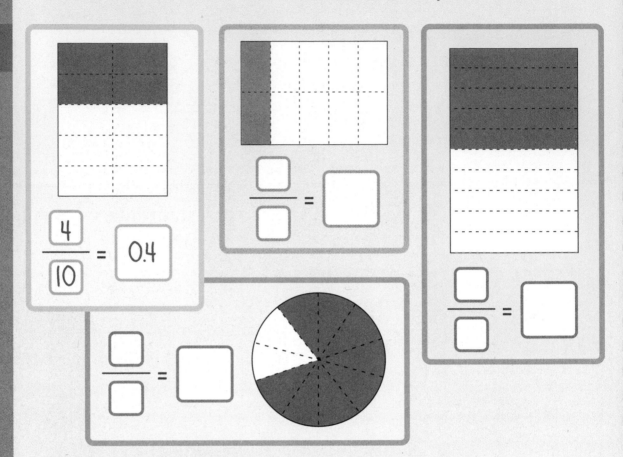

$$\frac{4}{10} = 0.4$$

Convert each fraction to a decimal.

$\dfrac{9}{10} =$ _____ | $\dfrac{1}{10} =$ _____ | $\dfrac{4}{10} =$ _____

$\dfrac{2}{10} =$ _____ | $\dfrac{5}{10} =$ _____ | $\dfrac{7}{10} =$ _____

BRAIN BOX

A **decimal** is a number that contains a decimal point followed by one or more digits to the right of the point.

The first digit to the right of the decimal point is in the **tenths place**.

Example: **0.8** ← tenths
↖ decimal point

0.8 tells us there are **8 tenths** or $\frac{8}{10}$

Convert each decimal to a fraction.

$0.6 = \dfrac{}{}$ | $0.8 = \dfrac{}{}$ | $0.1 = \dfrac{}{}$

This square has 100 equal parts.

What fraction of the square is shaded in?

Write your answer as a decimal. _____

Convert each fraction to a decimal.

$\dfrac{3}{100}$ = _0.03_ $\dfrac{2}{100}$ = _____

$\dfrac{5}{100}$ = _____ $\dfrac{9}{100}$ = _____

$\dfrac{8}{100}$ = _____ $\dfrac{6}{100}$ = _____

Convert each decimal to a fraction.

0.09 = $\dfrac{\boxed{}}{\boxed{}}$ | 0.01 = $\dfrac{\boxed{}}{\boxed{}}$ | 0.04 = $\dfrac{\boxed{}}{\boxed{}}$

BRAIN BOX

The second digit to the right of the decimal point is in the **hundredths place.**

tenths

Example: **0.08**

hundredths

0.08 tells us there are 8 hundredths or $\dfrac{8}{100}$

More to the Point

Answer the questions using the information on the card.

What is the place value of the **9** in the number above?

_____

Which digit is in the hundredths place? _____

Which digit is in the tens place? _____

What is the place value of the **5**? _____

How do you say this decimal aloud?
15.97 is **fifteen and ninety-seven hundredths.**

Thousandths

Answer each question.

28.346

tens   ones   decimal point   tenths   hundredths   thousandths

Decimal place values

What is the place value of the **6** in the number above?

_____

Write the number that says 8 tens, 5 ones, 3 tenths, 4 hundredths, 1 thousandth. _____

Which numeral is in the thousandths place in the number 3.862? _____

Write the number that says 3 tens, 2 ones, 4 tenths, 7 hundredths, 9 thousandths. _____

Write the decimal number for three and one hundredth.

_____

Write the number that says 4 tens, 0 ones, 0 tenths, 0 hundredths, 1 thousandth. _____

How do you say this decimal aloud? 28.346 is **twenty eight and three hundred, forty-six thousandths.**

Decimal Sums

Find the **sum**. Show your work.

Adding
decimals

$$5.6 + 1.2 = 6.8$$

$$7.3 + 6.6$$

$$3.7 + 2.8$$

$$8.17 + 2.3$$

$$9.14 + 3.73$$

$$4.25 + 3.71$$

$$4.85 + 3.22$$

$$6.38 + 2.17$$

$$8.49 + 2.45$$

$$5.33 + 6.27$$

$$9.75 + 1.82$$

$$7.64 + 1.85$$

BRAIN BOX

To **add decimals**, make sure that the decimal points are lined up. Add the numbers using the same strategy as you would with whole numbers—start with the column all the way to the right, which is the tenths column in this problem. Regroup if needed. Check that the decimal point stays in the same place.

$$
\begin{array}{r}
1 \\
5.63 \\
+\quad 4.85 \\
\hline
10.48
\end{array}
$$

Decimal Differences

Find the **difference**. Show your work.

Subtracting decimals

```
   4.8          7.3          3.99
 - 1.6        - 5.1        - 3.63
 ------       ------       -------
   3.2
```

```
   6.78         8.17         3.88
 - 2.33       - 3.04       - 1.29
 -------      -------      -------
```

```
   9.71         7.77         6.55
 - 4.52       - 2.83       - 3.29
 -------      -------      -------
```

```
   5.81         9.63         4.78
 - 1.77       - 4.82       - 2.96
 -------      -------      -------
```

BRAIN BOX

To **subtract decimals**, make sure that the decimal points are lined up. Subtract the numbers using the same strategy as you would with whole numbers—start with the column all the way to the right, which is the tenths column in this problem. Regroup if needed. Check that the decimal point stays in the same place.

```
   4 . 3 6
 - 2 . 1 4
 ----↓----
   2 . 2 2
```

Connecting the Dots

Connect each **fraction** in the left column with the equivalent **decimal** in the right column.

$\frac{13}{100}$	0.06
$\frac{6}{100}$	0.5
$\frac{5}{10}$	0.03
$\frac{3}{100}$	0.4
$\frac{4}{10}$	0.13
$\frac{1}{10}$	0.1
$\frac{1}{100}$	0.11
$\frac{7}{100}$	0.07
$\frac{6}{10}$	0.01
$\frac{11}{100}$	0.6

MEASUREMENT

How far away is your school? How tall are you? How much does your neighbor's dog weigh? You can measure to find the answers to these questions and more.

PARENTS Measurement is a practical application of math in our lives. Here's a quick way to talk about measurement with your child: make a pan of brownies and cut them into one-inch squares. Find the perimeter. Then find the area—it's the same as the number of brownies!

PLACE A STICKER HERE

For additional resources, visit www.BrainQuest.com/grade3

Is Your Foot a Foot Long?

Answer the questions about measuring **length**. Use the measurements below to help with your calculations.

36 inches (in) or 3 feet (ft) = **1 yard (yd)**

12 inches (in) = **1 foot (ft)**

1,760 yards (yds) or 5,280 feet (ft) = **1 mile (mi)**

Which unit of measurement would you use to measure:

- the length of your big toe _____

- the distance between two airports _____

- the height of an adult _____

Circle the best measurement for each.

the length of a worm

| 3 inches | 3 feet | 3 yards |

the height of a giraffe

| 15 inches | 15 feet | 15 miles |

the width of a house

| 7 inches | 7 feet | 7 yards |

the height of a door

| 7 inches | 7 feet | 7 miles |

the length of a football field

| 100 inches | 100 feet | 100 yards |

Write =, >, or < to show the relationship between each pair of measurements.

20 inches ☐ 2 feet

2 yards ☐ 72 inches

6 feet ☐ 3 yards

10 feet ☐ 120 inches

1 mile ☐ 5,000 feet

Customary linear measurements

Answer each question.

How many inches is 3 feet? _____

How many feet is 10 yards? _____

How many yards is 36 inches? _____

How many inches is 1 foot? _____

How many yards is 12 feet? _____

How many feet are in 2 miles? _____

BRAIN BOX

To show that two things have the same value, use the **equal** sign.

To show that a value is greater than another value, use the **greater than** sign.

To show that a value is less than another value, use the **less than** sign.

Example: 12 inches = 1 foot

Example: 3 feet > 2 feet

Example: 8 inches < 12 inches

How Long Is That Ant?

Answer the questions about measuring length using the metric system.

100 centimeters (cm) = 1 meter (m)

1,000 meters (m) = 1 kilometer (km)

Hint: Kilometers measure long distances, like the distance between cities.

Which unit of measurement would you use to measure:

- the length of a finger? _____
- the distance a plane travels? _____
- the height of a door? _____

Hint: Meters and yards measure similar lengths.

Circle the best measurement for each.

the length of a long distance race:

41 centimeters   41 meters   41 kilometers

the height of a basketball player:

2 centimeters   2 meters   2 kilometers

the length of a paper clip:

3 centimeters   3 meters   3 kilometers

the length of a rattlesnake:

$1\frac{1}{2}$ centimeters $1\frac{1}{2}$ meters $1\frac{1}{2}$ kilometers

Hint: A centimeter measures small things.

Customary vs. Metric

Cut out the ruler at the bottom of the page and measure each item below. Write the answers using customary and metric units of measurement.

Customary measurements

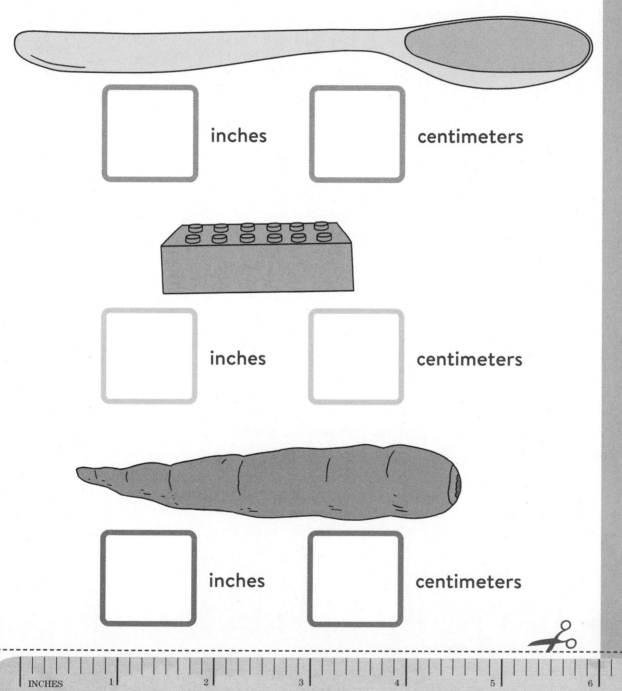

☐ inches   ☐ centimeters

☐ inches   ☐ centimeters

☐ inches   ☐ centimeters

INCHES | 1 | 2 | 3 | 4 | 5 | 6 | 7

CENTIMETERS | 18 | 17 | 16 | 15 | 14 | 13 | 12 | 11 | 10 | 9 | 8 | 7 | 6 | 5 | 4 | 3 | 2 | 1

The Mad Scientists

Answer the questions. Use the measurements below to help you with your calculations.

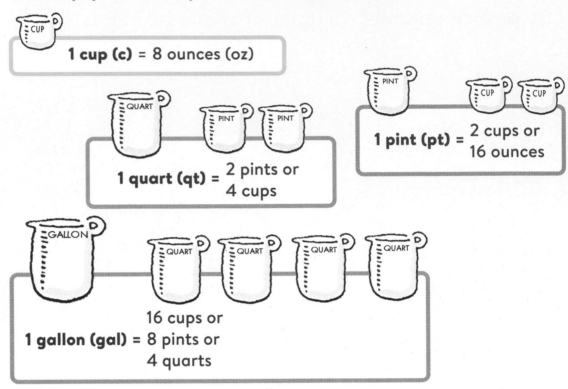

1 cup (c) = 8 ounces (oz)

1 quart (qt) = 2 pints or 4 cups

1 pint (pt) = 2 cups or 16 ounces

1 gallon (gal) = 16 cups or 8 pints or 4 quarts

Dr. Wack, the inventor, is making a hair removal tonic.

He needs 2 pints of swamp slime.
How many cups does he need? _____

His recipe calls for 4 gallons of mud.
How many quarts does he need? _____

Dr. Frank N. Stein is developing a cure for the common cold.

His formula calls for 16 ounces of melted cheese.
How many cups will he need? _____

He needs 4 quarts of snail ooze.
How many pints is that? _____

Now That's Heavy!

Write **ounces**, **pounds**, or **tons** to tell which unit of measurement you would use to measure each thing.

16 ounces (oz) = **1 pound (lb)**

2,000 pounds (lbs) = **1 ton**

Customary weight measurements

 a strawberry _____

a bicycle _____

 a flower _____

a dog _____

a dump truck _____

a boy _____

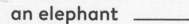 an elephant _____

Brain Quest Grade 3 Workbook

BRAIN BOX

Ounces, pounds, and **tons** are the customary units of measurement for **weight** in the United States.

Measuring Inside

Find the **area** of the figure.

MEASUREMENT

How many square units are inside this rectangle?

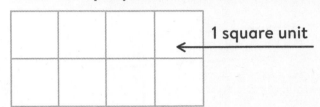

1 square unit

Area

That means the **area** of the rectangle is ___8___ square units.

Write the area below each figure.

_____
square units

_____
square units

_____
square units

_____
square units

_____
square units

_____
square units

BRAIN BOX

The area of a figure is the number of **square units** inside a figure.

Answer the questions.

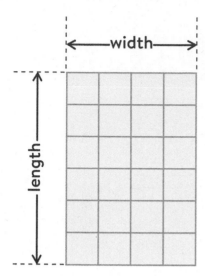

What is this figure's length?

_____ square units

What is this figure's width?

_____ square units

Area

The area of this figure = _____ × _____
                              width   length

What is the total area of this figure?

_____ square units

Write the area for each figure.

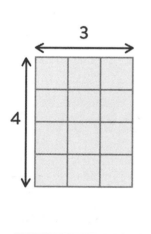

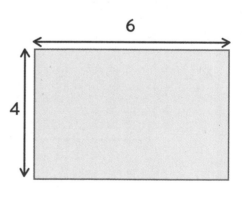

_____

square units

_____

square units

_____

square units

Matt has a poster of the wrestling star, the Brawler, which measures 7 feet long by 4 feet wide.

What is the area of his poster? _____

BRAIN BOX

You can find the area of a figure by multiplying its **length** by its **width**.

Let's Go Around

Write the **perimeter** below each geometric figure. Make sure to label your answer with either feet (ft) or inches (in).

Perimeters

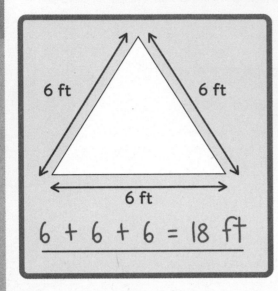

6 ft   6 ft

6 ft

6 + 6 + 6 = 18 ft

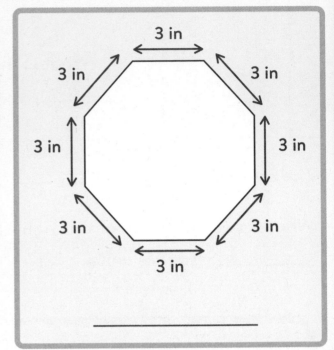

3 in

3 in   3 in

3 in   3 in

3 in   3 in

3 in

_____

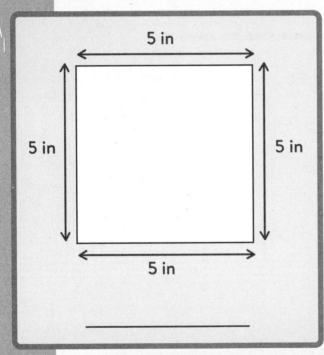

5 in

5 in   5 in

5 in

_____

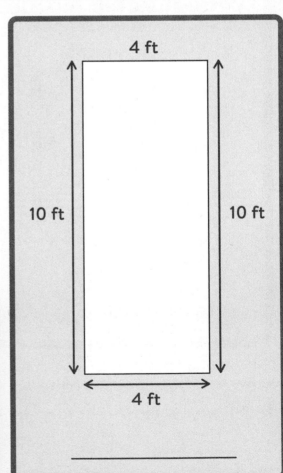

4 ft

10 ft   10 ft

4 ft

_____

BRAIN BOX

The **perimeter** is the distance around a figure. You can find the perimeter by adding the lengths of the sides.

For example:
This rug is 3 feet long and 1 foot wide. Its perimeter is 8 feet.

(3 + 3 + 1 + 1 = 8)

3 feet

1 foot   1 foot

3 feet

TIME AND MONEY

Did you know that telling time is a form of measuring? When you count hours, minutes, and seconds, you are measuring time. Let's do this—it's time to tell time!

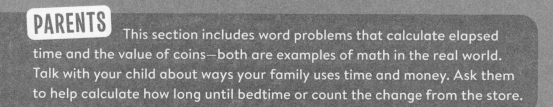

PARENTS This section includes word problems that calculate elapsed time and the value of coins—both are examples of math in the real world. Talk with your child about ways your family uses time and money. Ask them to help calculate how long until bedtime or count the change from the store.

PLACE A STICKER HERE

For additional resources, visit www.BrainQuest.com/grade3

It's About Time

Write the **time** below each clock.

| 24 hours = 1 day | 60 minutes = 1 hour | 60 seconds = 1 minute |

Telling time

6:00

 _____ : _____

 _____ : _____

 _____ : _____

 _____ : _____

 _____ : _____

 _____ : _____

 _____ : _____

_____ : _____

 _____ : _____

BRAIN BOX

Seconds, minutes, and hours are all measurements of time.

There are several ways to read time.

For example:
This clock shows
that the time is **4:50**.

You can also say or read the time as **50 minutes after four** or **10 minutes to five**.

 _____ : _____

 _____ : _____

 _____ : _____

Answer the questions.

It's 20 minutes to 7. How does a
digital clock show this time?

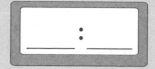

It's 7:30 a.m. How does a
digital clock show this time?

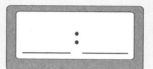

Rick's fastest time in the race was 50 seconds.
Nick's fastest time was 1 minute. Who was faster?

_____

How many hours are there between
11:00 a.m. on Monday and 11:00 a.m.
on Tuesday? _____

Luke and his friends went on a $1\frac{1}{2}$ hour hike.
How many minutes long was their hike? _____

Kate finished the race in $1\frac{1}{2}$ minutes.
What was her time in seconds? _____

BRAIN BOX

The hours between 12:00
midnight and 12:00 noon
are **a.m. hours.**

The hours between 12:00
noon and 12:00 midnight
are **p.m. hours.**

As Time Goes By

Answer the questions. Remember to include **a.m.** or **p.m.** in your answer if needed.

Elapsed time

Waldo the Wondrous started his magic show at 2:30 p.m. He finished his show at 4:00 p.m. How long was his show? _____

The Dynamites started baseball practice at 3:45 p.m. If practice lasted for 1 hour and 15 minutes, what time did it end? _____

Justin went to see a movie at Startime Cinema that was 2 hours and 5 minutes long. It started at 6:15 p.m. What time did it end? _____

The Bohidars ate pancakes from 8:15 a.m. to 9:00 a.m. How long were they eating pancakes?
_____

Raman's bowling party lasted for $1\frac{1}{2}$ hours. If it ended at 4:00 p.m., what time did it start?

_____

Rock Daddy's radio show is on from 10:30 a.m. until 11:45 a.m. How long is his show on?

_____

Elapsed time

The skating party at Roxie's Rollerdome started at 6:30 p.m. and ended at 8:15 p.m. How long did the party last? _____

Kenji went to the park at 10:00 a.m. and left at 11:55 a.m. How long was he at the park? _____

Bridget gave a 15-minute speech on her trip to Mexico. She finished her speech at 11:00 a.m. What time did she start her speech? _____

At 4:35 p.m., Bill Brawny got a flat tire. It took him 20 minutes to change the tire and get back on the road. At what time did he get back on the road? _____

Rosa's friends came over yesterday and stayed for 2 hours. If they left at 5:15 p.m., what time did they arrive? _____

The Money Tree

Coins are falling off the money tree!
How much money did these kids find?

BRAIN BOX

penny = 1¢

nickel = 5¢

dime = 10¢

quarter = 25¢

Connor found 2 nickels and 1 quarter.
How much did he find? _____

Kareem found 2 quarters, 5 dimes, and 5 pennies.
How much did he find? _____

Paul found 8 dimes, 4 nickels, and 1 quarter.
How much did he find? _____

Emily found 8 nickels. Laura found 2 dimes and
1 quarter. Who found more money? _____

Federico found 3 nickels, 6 dimes, and 2 quarters.
How much did he find? _____

Allison found 4 quarters and 4 dimes.
Denise found 10 nickels and 5 dimes.
Who found more money? _____

Add up the coins. Write the total sum on the line.

$1.05

_____

_____

_____

240

TIME AND MONEY

Adding and subtracting money

Yard Sale

Add and subtract using decimals.

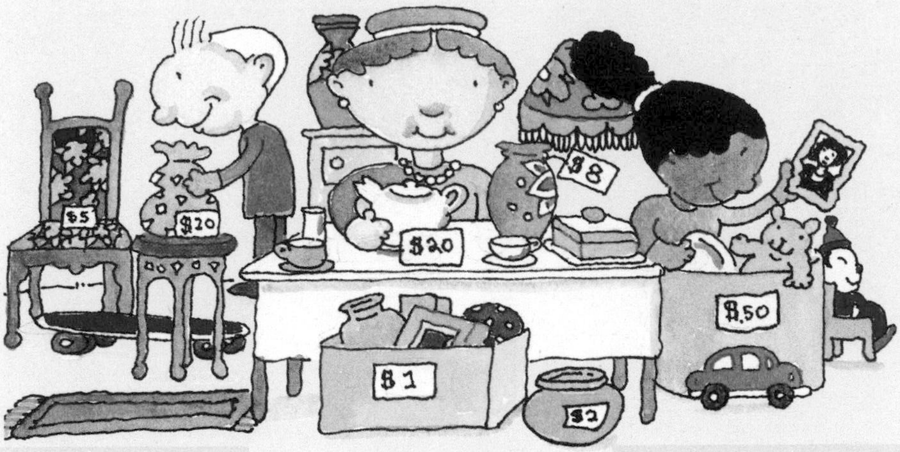

$3.57 + 0.12 $3.69	$3.00 + 0.42	$2.75 – 1.15
$3.54 – 0.44	$8.99 – 7.99	$9.99 + 2.99
$6.28 + 5.72	$6.50 – 1.30	$8.70 + 1.11
$5.24 – 3.83	$7.07 + 2.20	$7.31 – 6.69
$2.52 + 0.35	$4.95 – 4.93	$10.00 – 1.33

At the Amusement Park

Add and subtract using decimals. Use the extra space on the cards as your work area.

A ticket to ride on the Thunderbolt costs $1.50. How much will it cost Daryl and his sister to ride on this ride? __$3.00__

$$\begin{array}{r} \$1.50 \\ +\ 1.50 \\ \hline \$3.00 \end{array}$$

Using money

Cotton candy costs 60¢. Mrs. Gill bought one each for her son and her two daughters. She paid for them with $2.00. How much change should she get? _____

Diego bought four 80¢ tickets for rides on the Super Scorpion. How much did the tickets cost in all? _____

Melissa drove a bumper car for 75¢ and rode on the Ferris wheel for $1.25. How much did the rides cost? _____

The Whirl-a-Twirl costs $2.25. Takumi has 8 quarters and 2 dimes left. Does he have enough money for this ride? _____

Zoo Gift Shop

Ariana's third-grade class bought souvenirs when they went to the zoo. Subtract using decimals to figure out how much change each student received.

Making change

$5.95

Paid $6.00
    -5.95
    0.05

$1.29

Paid $2.00

$9.99

Paid $10.00

_____

$3.47

Paid $4.00

_____

$8.25

Paid $9.00

_____

$1.35

Paid $5.00

_____

$5.97

Paid $10.00

_____

$7.00

Paid $8.00

_____

$4.63

Paid $5.00

_____

WORD PROBLEMS

Sometimes, math problems are more than just numbers. Word problems tell stories about numbers, and it's your job to find the solutions. Let's start solving!

PARENTS These addition, subtraction, multiplication, and division word problems are opportunities for your learner to see math applied in realistic situations. Challenge your child to check their work using different strategies. Remind them that finding mistakes and fixing them is a powerful way to learn.

PLACE A STICKER HERE

All Together Now

Solve each **addition word problem.** Use the extra space on the cards as your work area. Write the answer in the white box.

There are 45 girls in the pool and 36 boys in the pool. How many children in all are in the pool?

$$\begin{array}{r} 1 \\ 45 \\ + 36 \\ \hline 81 \end{array}$$

81

Farmer Dell has 45 cows and 20 pigs. How many cows and pigs does he have altogether?

Aaron and his brother went fishing. Aaron caught 15 fish. His brother caught 9 fish. How many fish did they catch in all?

The balloon seller has 10 red balloons, 12 blue balloons, 8 yellow balloons, and 6 green balloons. How many balloons does he have altogether?

BRAIN BOX

In word problems that ask about the **total** of two or more things, you need to **add.**

Solve the **addition word problems.**

Our school library had 55 biographies. The librarian just bought 19 more. A local bookstore donated another 31 biographies. What is the total number of biographies in the school library now?

Tamika swam 10 laps in the pool on Monday and 15 laps on Tuesday. Tony swam 18 laps on Wednesday and 20 laps on Thursday. How many laps did Tamika and Tony swim altogether by the end of the week?

Now it's time to write your own problem! Write an **addition word problem** and give it to a friend to solve.

Subtract It!

Solve each **subtraction word problem.** Use the extra space on the card as your work area. Write your answer in the white box.

Dulce sold 35 boxes of cookies for her Girl Scout troop. Meredith sold 47 boxes of Girl Scout cookies. How many more boxes of cookies did Meredith sell?

Rita bought a box of raisins with 88 raisins in it. She ate 26 of the raisins before passing the box to her friend Kaylee. Kaylee ate 41 raisins. How many raisins are left in the box?

Gina ran the race in 72 seconds. Kristina ran the race in 85 seconds. What was the difference between their times?

Aunt Linda put 38 gumdrops in her candy dish. Samantha grabbed 9 when she stopped by after school. Uncle Jeff ate 10 for dessert. Aunt Linda snacked on 2 before she went to bed. How many gumdrops are left?

BRAIN BOX

In word problems that ask about the **difference** between two numbers, you need to **subtract.**

Solve the **subtraction word problems.**

Haji has a collection of 86 baseball cards. Ethan has 100 baseball cards in his collection. How many more baseball cards does Ethan have?

Mr. Shah is driving across the country. On Monday, he drove 320 miles. On Tuesday, he drove 375 miles. How many fewer miles did he drive on Monday?

Jake wants to earn $130 this summer. He has earned $75 so far. How many more dollars does he have to earn to meet his goal?

Write your own **subtraction word problem.** Then give it to a friend to solve!

Get a Clue

Solve each **division word problem.** Use the extra space on the card as your work area. Write the answer in the white box.

Division

Akila divided her 55 dimes evenly into 5 piles. How many dimes did she put in each pile?

Gabby's Goofy Gifts has 81 windup mice. They are packed with 9 in each box. How many boxes of windup mice do they have?

There are 24 cookies in the cookie jar. If 8 girls share the cookies equally, how many cookies will each girl get?

Alexis has 56 pumpkin seeds. She has made 8 rows and wants to plant the same number of seeds in each row. How many pumpkin seeds should she put in each row?

A Multitude of Math

Solve each **multiplication word problem.** Use the extra space on the card as your work area. Write the answer in the white box.

Multiplication

You are going on a road trip. Your car can travel 50 miles in 1 hour. How many miles can it travel in 4 hours?

You need a play mat that covers the patio in your back yard. The patio is 9 feet wide and 6 feet long. How many feet total does the play mat need to be?

Your cat has 12 whiskers on each cheek. How many whiskers does it have on both cheeks?

It takes 42 building bricks to make one castle. How many bricks will you need to be able to make 5 castles?

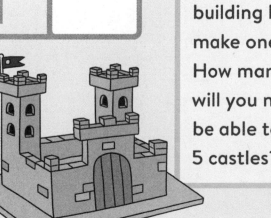

Brain Quest Grade 3 Workbook

Which Operation?

Solve each **word problem** using **addition**, **subtraction**, **multiplication**, or **division**. First write which operation you are going to use in the long yellow box. Then solve the problem and write your answer in the white box.

The Snack Shack sold 87 bags of pretzels on Saturday and 65 bags of pretzels on Sunday. How many more bags of pretzels did they sell on Saturday?

$$\begin{array}{r} 87 \\ -\ 65 \\ \hline 22 \end{array}$$

subtraction | 22

There are 9 tables in Mr. Lyden's art room. If there are 5 students at each table, how many students are at the tables?

At the school bake sale, Sam sold 26 banana muffins and 34 cranberry muffins. How many muffins in all did they sell?

Gracie makes bracelets. She uses 9 beads in each bracelet she makes. How many bracelets can she make with 72 beads?

BRAIN BOX

Word problems have clue words and phrases that tell you what operation you need to do to solve the problem.

Addition	Subtraction	Multiplication	Division
• how many	• how many more	• how many	• each
• total number	• how many less		• every
• in all	• how many are left		
• altogether	• what is the difference		

Don't Forget to Vote!

It's election day at school! Solve the word problems using either **addition**, **subtraction**, **multiplication**, or **division**.

Mixed operation problems

In the election for class president, Anu received 64 votes and Scott received 46 votes. By how many votes did Anu win the election?

In the run for vice president, Lydia got 20 votes. Gabrielle got 4 times as many votes as Lydia did. How many votes did Gabrielle get?

Shayla spent 12 hours campaigning for class secretary. Her opponent spent 4 more hours campaigning than she did. How many hours did Shalya's opponent spend campaigning?

Lucas won the election for class treasurer by promising to raise $25 for class field trips. If the field-trip fund already has $25 in it, how much will it be if Lucas keeps his promise?

Challenge Yourself!

Find the information needed to solve each problem, write an equation, and solve it. (Hint: There might be more information than you need!)

Word problems

A school supplies box holds 20 items: 5 crayons, 4 index cards, 3 markers, 2 glue sticks, 1 pair of scissors. The rest of the items are pencils. How many pencils are in the box?

> 5 crayons + 4 index cards + 3 markers + 2 glue sticks
> + 1 pair of scissors = 15 items
> 20 items total − 15 items = **5 pencils**

When Julissa was 10 years old, her little brother, Pedro, was half her age. When Julissa is 18 years old, how old will Pedro be?

Ms. Edwards put one stack of paper on 10 different desks. Each stack had 3 pieces of yellow paper, 3 pieces of blue paper, and 3 pieces of green paper. How many pieces of paper were there altogether?

The third grade hosted a food drive for 3 weeks. Students collected a total of 64 cans and 36 boxes of food. If they divide the total number of cans and boxes they collected among 4 different organizations, how many items will each organization receive?

SOCIAL STUDIES

How many states can you name? What are the three branches of government? Let's learn about government and history.

PARENTS Social studies isn't all maps and place names. Social studies encompasses learning about the world near and far, from government and economics to historical figures and important events. Extend your child's learning by helping them research topics they're interested in online or in books.

PLACE A
STICKER
HERE

This Land Is Your Land

Use the map of the United States to answer the questions on the next few pages.

Regions of the US

- Northeast
- Southeast
- Midwest
- Southwest
- West

Which state is directly east of Indiana?_____

    North of Indiana?_____

    West of Indiana?_____

    South of Indiana?_____

Which state is directly north of Arkansas?_____

Which states border Iowa?

_____   _____   _____

_____   _____   _____

Which state is bordered by only one other state?

_____

In what region is your state located?_____

Which state is directly west of North Dakota?_____

What four states have corners that all touch in the same exact place? (HINT: these corners form the shape of a **+**.)

_____   _____

_____   _____

Which state is directly south of Nebraska?_____

How many states have the word **North** in their names? _____

Write them: _____

How many states have the word **West** in their names? _____

Write them: _____

Size Wise

Look at these two charts and the map on page 254 to answer the questions below.

Top 10 Largest States in Total Area (Land and Water)

1.	Alaska	663,267 square miles
2.	Texas	268,581 square miles
3.	California	163,696 square miles
4.	Montana	147,042 square miles
5.	New Mexico	121,589 square miles
6.	Arizona	113,998 square miles
7.	Nevada	110,561 square miles
8.	Colorado	104,094 square miles
9.	Oregon	98,381 square miles
10.	Wyoming	97,814 square miles

Top 10 Smallest States in Total Area (Land and Water)

1.	Rhode Island	1,545 square miles
2.	Delaware	2,489 square miles
3.	Connecticut	5,543 square miles
4.	New Jersey	8,721 square miles
5.	New Hampshire	9,350 square miles
6.	Vermont	9,614 square miles
7.	Massachusetts	10,555 square miles
8.	Hawai'i	10,931 square miles
9.	Maryland	12,407 square miles
10.	West Virginia	24,230 square miles

Which two states are the largest?

_____ _____

Which two states are the smallest?

_____ _____

Which two northeastern states have an area between 9,000 and 10,000 square miles?

_____ _____

The top 10 biggest states are all located in the western US.

True or false? _____

Which small state is an island chain? _____

Play Ball

Below each baseball jersey, write the name of the state in which the team can be found.

Cities and states

Houston Astros

_____

Boston Red Sox

_____

Atlanta Braves

_____

Seattle Mariners

_____

Milwaukee Brewers

_____

Chicago Cubs

_____

Philadelphia Phillies

_____

Cleveland Guardians

_____

Los Angeles Dodgers

_____

St. Louis Cardinals

_____

Baltimore Orioles

_____

Pittsburgh Pirates

_____

Your Home State!

Answer these questions about where you live. You may need to do some research in an atlas, another reference book, or online.

What state do you live in?

_____

What is the capital of your state?

_____

What is the population of your state?

_____

What are three of the major industries of your state?

_____

_____

_____

Draw the shape of your state:

What states border your state?

_____

What is your state bird?

_____

Your state

What is your state flower?

_____

Draw your state flag:

Shorten It Up

Each state in the United States has a two-letter postal abbreviation for its name. Use the map to write the postal abbreviation for every state.

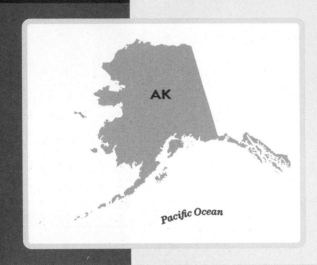

Alabama _____   Colorado _____

Alaska _____   Connecticut _____

Arizona _____   Delaware _____

Arkansas _____   Florida _____

California _____ Georgia _____

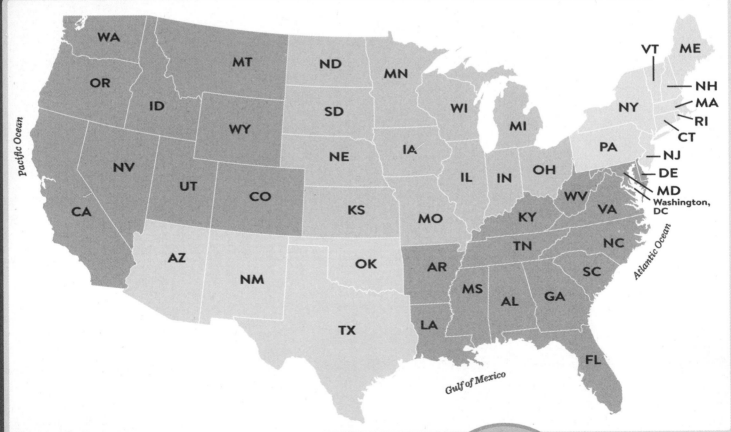

State
abbreviations

Hawai'i _____

Idaho _____

Illinois _____

Indiana _____

Iowa _____

Kansas _____

Kentucky _____

Louisiana _____

Maine _____

Maryland _____

Massachusetts _____

Michigan _____

Minnesota _____

Mississippi _____

Missouri _____

Montana _____

Nebraska _____

Nevada _____

New Hampshire _____

New Jersey _____

New Mexico _____

New York _____

North Carolina _____

North Dakota _____

Ohio _____

Oklahoma _____

Oregon _____

Pennsylvania _____

Rhode Island _____

South Carolina _____

South Dakota _____

Tennessee _____

Texas _____

Utah _____

Vermont _____

Virginia _____

Washington _____

West Virginia _____

Wisconsin _____

Wyoming _____

The capital of the United States is _____.

What do the last two letters stand for? _____

We the People . . .

The Constitution

The US constitution is a set of laws that describes the rights of US citizens and how the US government works. The men who wrote the Constitution decided the United States should be a democracy, a type of government where leaders are elected by the people, through voting.

The laws laid out in the Constitution protect people's rights to freedom, and their right to rule their own country. The Bill of Rights is the group of amendments added to the Constitution in 1791 that name individual rights of American citizens, including the freedom of speech, freedom of religion, and the right to a fair trial.

The first three words of the constitution are "We the people. . . ." That's because the Constitution was written to represent the voices of all people, not just the powerful leaders. However, at the time, "We the people" did not mean everyone in the US. The rules in the Constitution only applied to white men. Women of all races, Black men, and Indigenous men were not allowed to vote and were not offered equal protections by the US Constitution.

In time, amendments were added to the Constitution that protected the rights of all citizens, regardless of race or gender.

What is the US Constitution?

_____

_____

_____

What type of government is the United States?

_____

How are government leaders chosen in a democracy?

_____

_____

_____

Who was allowed to participate in democracy when
the US Constitution was written? Who was excluded?

_____

_____

_____

Name two freedoms that the Bill of Rights protects.

_____

_____

_____

The US Government

The Three Branches of Government

The United States has three branches of government: the executive branch, the legislative branch, and the judicial branch. Each branch holds equal but separate power so that there is a system of checks and balances.

The **executive branch** is headed by the president and includes the vice president and the fifteen presidential advisors that make up the Cabinet. The main job of the executive branch is to protect and serve the citizens of the United States by enforcing the laws.

The **legislative branch** is headed by Congress. Its job is to create the laws that govern the people. Congress is made up of two parts: the Senate and the House of Representatives. The Senate has one hundred senators: two for every state—no matter how big or small the state. In the House of Representatives, the number of members per state varies according to state population. A state with a large population has more representatives than a state with a small population.

The **judicial branch** is responsible for interpreting the laws of the Constitution to make sure everyone is being treated fairly. The Supreme Court of the judicial branch is the highest court in the US, and everyone—even the president!—must accept its rulings.

Name the three branches of government.

_____

Why does the government have three branches of government
instead of one?

_____

_____

Who is in charge of the executive branch?

_____

Which two legislative groups make up Congress?

_____

_____

How many senators are in the Senate? How many senators
does each state have?

_____

What is the highest court in the United States?

_____

Why do you think smaller states have fewer representatives
than larger states in the House?

_____

The US
government

Women and the Vote

This time line shows some important events in the history of the **women's suffrage movement** in the United States. Use it to answer the questions below.

Understanding time lines

1851
Sojourner Truth, a formerly enslaved abolitionist and women's rights activist, delivers the now-famous speech "Ain't I a Woman?" at a women's rights convention in Akron, Ohio.

1890
Wyoming becomes the first state to grant women the right to vote.

1840　　1850　　1860　　1870　　1880　　1890　　1900

1848
The first women's rights convention in the US is held in Seneca Falls, NY.

1866
Susan B. Anthony, Elizabeth Cady Stanton, and others found the American Equal Rights Association, which petitions Congress for "universal suffrage"— voting rights for citizens of any gender.

1896
Mary Church Terrell, Harriet Tubman, and Ida B. Wells found The National Association of Colored Women to advocate for rights for women of color, who were often excluded from other women's rights groups.

In which year did Sojourner Truth deliver the speech called "Ain't I a Woman?"? _____

Which state elected the first woman to the House of Representatives? _____

Was Jeannette Rankin elected before or after women had the right to vote? _____

BRAIN BOX

The women's suffrage movement was the fight to win women the right to vote.

Understanding
time lines

1965
The Voting Rights Act
outlaws discriminatory
voting practices (like
literacy tests and poll
taxes), empowering
women of color to exercise
their right to vote.

1916
Jeannette Rankin of Montana
becomes the first woman elected
to the House of Representatives.

| 1910 | 1920 | 1930 | 1940 | 1950 | 1960 | 1970 |

1920
The Nineteenth Amendment
grants women the right to
vote, though many women
of color will continue to face
barriers when trying to do so.

Sojourner Truth

In 1920, were all women in the US able to freely exercise
their right to vote? Why or why not?

_____

_____

_____

What did the Voting Rights Act of 1965 prohibit?

_____

_____

_____

Going to Washington

Washington, DC, is the capital of the United States and the home of the three branches of government. Circle the twelve government words hidden in the puzzle. The words go across and down.

Government word search

legislative	Capitol	term	White House
federal	Congress	Senate	president
government	state	representative	law

G	O	V	E	R	N	M	E	N	T	K	F	D	A	U	B
X	C	O	N	G	R	E	S	S	G	C	X	O	I	P	R
R	B	B	E	U	O	F	Q	C	Y	E	R	F	E	R	G
E	J	L	E	G	I	S	L	A	T	I	V	E	I	E	D
P	E	P	G	B	Q	J	D	P	S	H	B	Z	M	S	O
R	M	A	K	Y	X	A	S	I	C	Y	P	H	C	I	S
E	Z	H	M	C	U	H	R	T	H	U	E	Z	Y	D	J
S	S	W	H	I	T	E	H	O	U	S	E	J	O	E	Z
E	D	R	Q	M	Y	B	I	L	B	Z	A	Z	P	N	Q
N	Z	X	Z	A	F	Z	F	E	M	S	E	N	A	T	E
T	H	F	G	Y	E	A	R	O	M	T	U	D	S	H	D
A	F	R	Q	C	D	U	D	X	Z	A	S	Z	F	Z	B
T	E	R	M	Z	E	R	E	C	J	T	Z	X	J	E	U
I	P	G	R	O	R	G	K	H	Q	E	K	A	M	B	K
V	A	X	I	L	A	W	Z	Z	F	B	E	Z	D	Q	G
E	O	B	Y	I	L	U	E	D	Q	A	A	S	U	Q	X

SCIENCE

What do mammals, reptiles, amphibians, birds, and fish have in common? They're all animals, of course! But how are they alike, and how are they different? Where do they live and what do they eat? Let's turn the page to learn more about our world!

PARENTS In this section, third graders will explore concepts of earth, life, and physical sciences that are foundational to their scientific learning. Help your child think like a scientist. Encourage them to ask questions that spring from content they read. And if you can't answer a question, it's great to say, "I don't know, but let's find out!"

PLACE A STICKER HERE

Information, Please

Look at the information that is usually found in reference books. These pages are from a book about amphibians.

The **table of contents** tells you the titles of the chapters in the book and the page on which each chapter begins.

CONTENTS

A **glossary** is an alphabetical listing that gives the meanings of some words that are used in the book.

GLOSSARY

caecilian   a wormlike amphibian that lives underground

cold-blooded   having a body temperature that changes with that of the surrounding air or water temperature

An **index** is an alphabetical listing that tells where you can find a particular subject.

INDEX

Answer the questions.

In which chapter should you look to find out about "colorful" amphibians? _____

On which page does the first chapter of the book begin? _____

In which chapter would you look to find out about how amphibians breathe? _____

If you want to find out about tadpoles, on which page would you begin looking? _____

Where would you look to find out what general subjects the reference book covers? _____

Where would you look to find out on which page or pages a particular person, place, or subject is covered? _____

Where would you look to find out the meaning of an unfamiliar word or term? _____

Flutter in the Air

Read the passage.

Butterflies and Moths

Butterflies and moths are beautiful insects. They belong to the same group of insects, which is called *Lepidoptera*. Like all insects, butterflies and moths have six legs. But unlike other insects, they have scales that cover their wings. Both moths and butterflies have two pairs of wings. That's four wings in all.

Butterflies and moths go through four stages of development:

- **Egg:** Females usually lay their eggs on a leaf or a stem.
- **Caterpillar:** A caterpillar eats and eats. It sheds its skin several times as it grows.
- **Pupa:** The caterpillar rests in either a chrysalis, if it's a butterfly, or a cocoon, if it's a moth. This hard shell protects it.
- **Adult:** When the pupa cracks, the adult butterfly or moth emerges.

All butterflies and moths undergo this metamorphosis, or transformation, from egg to adult. Butterflies and moths also differ in several ways. Most butterflies have slender, hairless bodies. Most moths have plump, furry bodies. Many butterflies are brightly colored, while many moths have a dull color. Most butterflies fly during the day, while most moths fly at night. A butterfly's antennae are knobbed at the tips. A moth's antennae are plain or feathery at the tips. Most butterflies hold their wings upright over their backs while they are resting, but most moths rest with their wings stretched out flat.

Some species of moths and butterflies migrate. That means that they make a journey to a new place. One of the most amazing migrations is made by the monarch butterfly, which flies south to find a new home for the winter. Millions of monarchs fly thousands of miles to reach forests of fir trees in Mexico. There they rest and feed after their long journey.

Name the four stages of development in the life cycle of moths and butterflies.

1. _____   3. _____

2. _____   4. _____

Define these terms.

Lepidoptera: _____

migrate: _____

Fill in this Venn diagram.

Write two ways that moths are different from butterflies.

Write two ways that butterflies and moths are the same.

Write two ways that most butterflies are different from moths.

moths   both   butterflies

We've Got Backbones

Read the passage.

Creature Features

Animals that have backbones are called vertebrates. Vertebrates include five classes of animals:

- **Mammals:** Mammals are warm-blooded animals with hair. All mammals feed their young with milk. Some examples are people, dogs, mice, dolphins, whales, horses, and chimpanzees.

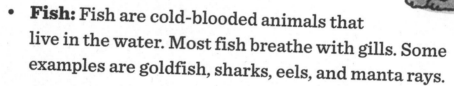

- **Fish:** Fish are cold-blooded animals that live in the water. Most fish breathe with gills. Some examples are goldfish, sharks, eels, and manta rays.

- **Birds:** Birds are warm-blooded animals that have wings, feathers, and beaks. Most birds can fly. Some examples are hawks, barn owls, toucans, eagles, and swans.

- **Amphibians:** Amphibians are cold-blooded animals that live in the water and breathe with gills at the beginning of their lives. Later, they move onto land and breathe with lungs for the rest of their life. Some examples are salamanders, frogs, and toads.

- **Reptiles:** Reptiles are cold-blooded animals that have scales and lay eggs. Some examples are geckos, crocodiles, boa constrictors, snakes, chameleons, and sea turtles.

Using what you learned about vertebrates, list three examples of each class of animal.

birds

_____

_____

_____

mammals

_____

_____

_____

amphibians

_____

_____

_____

Vertebrates

reptiles

_____

_____

_____

fish

_____

_____

_____

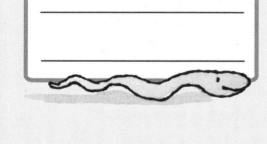

Fill in the chart, checking off **warm-blooded** or **cold-blooded** for each class of vertebrate.

	mammals	birds	amphibians	reptiles	fish
warm-blooded					
cold-blooded					

Feathered Friends

Read about birds. Then answer the questions.

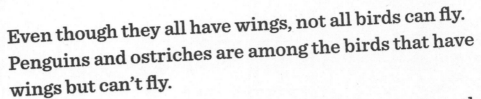

Even though they all have wings, not all birds can fly. Penguins and ostriches are among the birds that have wings but can't fly.

Whether they eat meat or plants, birds do not chew their food—that's because they have no teeth! Birds use their beak or their claws to gather food. Birds of prey, such as hawks, eagles, and owls, spot small animals on the ground to hunt from high above in their perch. Other birds eat seeds and drink nectar from plants.

Many birds fly south for the winter to stay warm, and head north in the summer to stay cool. This is called migration.

Name a bird that doesn't fly.

_____

Many birds fly south for the winter. What is this called?

_____

Why don't birds chew their food?

_____

Name three types of birds of prey.

_____

Read the **essay** about owls.
Then answer the questions.

Birds

Many people have never seen an owl in the wild. That's because owls are usually quiet and motionless as they roost during the day. It is at night that they become active, for this is when they hunt for their prey.

Owls are well equipped for hunting. Their huge eyes can see well in the dark, and their hearing is very sensitive. Soft-fringed feathers on their wings help them fly so quietly that most animals don't hear them coming. To catch and carry their prey, owls have needle-sharp claws called talons. Owls usually swallow their prey whole. Parts that can't be digested—hair, teeth, feathers, and bones—are spit up in pellets.

Name four things that help the owl hunt its prey.

1. _____

2. _____

3. _____

4. _____

What happens to the parts of the prey that the owl's stomach can't digest?

_____

Something's Fishy

Read about fish. Then answer the questions.

Fish

Fish do not have lungs. They take in oxygen through their gills. Unlike mammals, fish must be underwater in order to breathe. Most fish are covered with scales, and they have several fins and a strong tail, which help them swim through the water.

You can find fish in just about any body of water—oceans, streams, lakes, rivers, ponds—both in salt water and fresh water. Some fish stay by themselves, but many live in a large group called a school. Many fish eat other fish or smaller sea creatures, while others survive on a diet of underwater plants called algae.

Do fish use lungs or gills to breathe? _____

What covers the body of most fish? _____

What is a large group of fish called? _____

What two body parts do fish use to help them move through the water?

_____

What do some fish eat, other than underwater plants?

_____

Scary or Scaly

Read about reptiles. Then answer the questions.

While not all reptiles are dangerous, some are. The boa constrictor is a long, powerful snake that wraps itself around its prey and squeezes it to death. Poisonous snakes such as rattlesnakes and cobras inject their poison into their prey through their sharp teeth or fangs.

Many people confuse two similar reptiles: alligators and crocodiles. Although they look alike, there are some differences. When a crocodile has its mouth closed, you can still see all of its teeth. When an alligator's mouth is closed, you can see only its top teeth. An alligator's snout is wider than a crocodile's. Lastly, alligators are found mostly in the southeastern United States. Crocodiles live on almost every continent.

Name two kinds of poisonous snakes.

1. _____

2. _____

Name three differences between alligators and crocodiles.

1. _____

2. _____

3. _____

Take Me Home

Read about animal habitats. Then draw a line from each animal to its habitat.

An animal's habitat is the place where it naturally lives and grows. The habitat provides everything the animal needs: food, shelter, the right temperature, and protection.

giraffe

cheetah

parrot

whale

deer

shark

octopus

woodpecker

buffalo

squirrel

toucan

zebra

WOODLAND

RAIN FOREST

GRASSLAND

OCEAN

Help!

Draw a line from each animal to the card that describes how it protects itself.

 turtle

 squid

 chameleon

 poison dart frog

 skunk

 moose

 cheetah

puffer fish

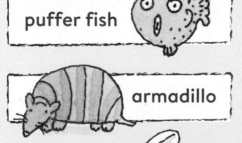 armadillo

wasp

runs away very fast

is brightly colored to warn that it is poisonous

rolls up into a ball

shoots inky liquid to hide itself

has a poison stinger

sprays out a smelly substance

puffs itself up so it's too big for predators to swallow

has large antlers as weapons

changes colors to camouflage itself

hides in its shell

The Human Body

Draw a line from the system on the left to the part of the body that belongs to that system.

The body's organs work together in groups known as systems. Each of these systems has an important set of functions to perform.

digestive system:
responsible for getting food in and out of the body

respiratory system:
responsible for breathing

muscular system:
responsible for movement

sensory system:
responsible for seeing, hearing, tasting, touching, and smelling

skeletal system:
responsible for bones and joints that support and protect the body

circulatory system:
responsible for getting blood to all the parts of the body

nervous system:
controls all the functions of the body

brain

ears

blood

lungs

stomach

biceps

spine

The Human Skeleton

Read about bones. Then answer the questions.

There are 206 bones in the human body. These bones are connected to each other at joints. The bones and joints make up the human skeleton, which is what supports and protects the human body. For instance, the skull protects the brain. The ribs protect the heart and lungs.

Half the bones in the human body are in the hands and feet. The smallest bone is in the ear. The biggest bone is in the thigh.

Bones are held together by ligaments, and they move with the help of muscles. When babies are born, their bones are still soft. This soft bone is called cartilage. As babies grow, the cartilage hardens into bone. Calcium, a mineral found in milk and eggs and broccoli, helps make bones stronger.

How many bones are there in the human body?

_____

How many bones are in the hands and feet?

_____

What part of the body does the skull protect?

_____

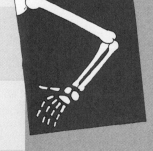

What holds bones together?

_____

What is found in milk, eggs, and broccoli that is good for bones?

_____

Keep Your Balance!

Look at the two pictures below. Then fill in the blanks using the words in the Word Boxes.

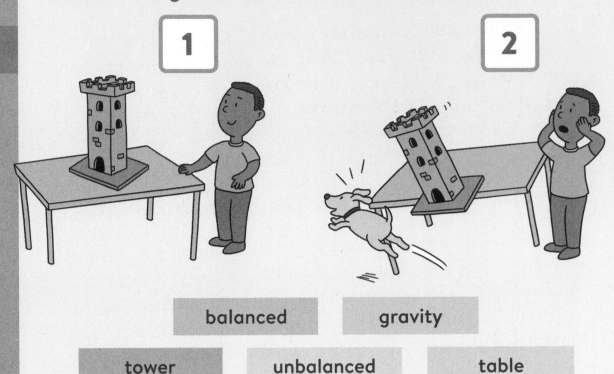

1

2

balanced	gravity

tower	unbalanced	table

The forces in Picture 1 are _____.

The forces in Picture 2 are _____.

In Picture 1, the _____ is pushing up on the tower.

In Picture 1, the _____ is pushing down on the table.

In Picture 2, the force of _____ is pulling the tower toward the floor.

BRAIN BOX

A **force** is something that pushes or pulls. **Gravity** is an example of a force that pulls objects down. Forces acting on an object can be either balanced or unbalanced. When forces are **balanced**, there is no change in an object's speed or direction. But when the forces acting on an object are **unbalanced**, this can cause an object to move or to change its speed or its direction.

Look at the pictures. Circle whether the forces are balanced or unbalanced.

Balanced and unbalanced forces

balanced   unbalanced

balanced   unbalanced

balanced   unbalanced

balanced   unbalanced

balanced   unbalanced

balanced   unbalanced

Which Weather?

Use the seven-day weather forecast to answer the questions.

Sunday	Monday	Tuesday	Wednesday	Thursday	Friday	Saturday
High: 51 °F	High: 48 °F	High: 32 °F	High: 41 °F	High: 54 °F	High: 61 °F	High: 55 °F
Low: 36 °F	Low: 35 °F	Low: 24 °F	Low: 30 °F	Low: 42 °F	Low: 49 °F	Low: 43 °F
Chance of rain: 100%	Chance of rain: 40%	Chance of snow: 80%	Chance of rain: 15%	Chance of rain: 60%	Chance of rain: 5%	Chance of rain: 90%

Which is the only day this week in which snow is predicted?

_____

On which three days are the high temperatures forecasted to be in the 50s?

_____

Which day is predicted to have a low temperature in the 20s?

_____

On which day are forecasters certain there will be rain?

_____

On which day are you least likely to need an umbrella?

_____

BRAIN BOX

We can use **percentage** to say how likely something—such as rain—is to happen. The higher the percentage, or the closer the percentage is to 100, the more likely something is to happen.

Weather Log!

What's the weather where you are? Use this weather tracker to record conditions around you over a five-day period. Use the weather column to draw a picture of or write about the weather. Ask a grown-up to help you find out the daily temperature.

DAY	WEATHER	TEMPERATURE
Day 1 Date:		High: Low:
Day 2 Date:		High: Low:
Day 3 Date:		High: Low:
Day 4 Date:		High: Low:
Day 5 Date:		High: Low:

Which day had the highest temperature you recorded?

_____

Which day had the lowest? _____

How many days of sun did you have? _____

How many days of rain? _____

How Magnetic!

Magnets have two poles: a north pole and a south pole. When two magnets are placed near each other, their poles have a force that will either pull the two magnets together or push the two magnets apart. If the poles are the same, they will push apart (be repelled). If the poles are different, they will pull together (be attracted).

Will these two magnets pull together or push apart?

| N | S | | N | S |

_____

Will these two magnets pull together or push apart?

| N | S | | S | N |

_____

Magnets can attract or pick up many metal objects. Put an M in front of objects that are attracted or can be picked up by a magnet.

_____ paper clip   _____ safety pin

_____ plastic fork   _____ rubber band

_____ candle   _____ nail

_____ bolt   _____ crayon

_____ metal spoon

TECHNOLOGY

Computers follow algorithms, which are directions written in code. People who write code are called programmers. Ready to think like a programmer?

PARENTS Algorithms can be as simple as a set of directions, like a recipe. They can also be complex, like a long computer program made of thousands of lines of code. In this section, your child will learn about the importance of a strong password, how to follow algorithms, and how to write basic code.

PLACE A STICKER HERE

For additional resources, visit www.BrainQuest.com/grade3

Petra's Note

Petra typed a note to her friend Janita.

Dear janita,

Howare you I am
practicing typing.

I hhhope you have
a good day today!

Your friend,

Petra

This note has some mistakes. Can you find them?

1. Circle the word where Petra should have used the Delete or Backspace key.

2. Draw a star next to the word where Petra forgot to use the Shift key.

3. Underline the part of the note where Petra didn't use the space bar.

4. Draw an arrow where Petra forgot a question mark.

5. Draw a rectangle around the word that is in a different font.

Power Passwords!

A password should be hard for others to guess. Read how to make powerful passwords. Don't forget to keep your password private from everyone but trusted adults!

Cybersecurity and passwords

DO:

- make sure you use at least eight characters
- mix it up: use numbers, letters (upper and lowercase), and symbols

DON'T:

- use your birthday, your pet's name, or anything else about you as part of your password
- share your password with anyone else (except a trusted adult)

Can you pick a powerful password?
Circle the strong passwords.

abc123

mypassword

MyDogMax

I_L0ve_2C0d3

C@tsAr3C00l!

12345678

Bra1n@Qu3st21

QWERTYUI

BRAIN BOX

A **password** is a secret group of letters, numbers, and symbols that allow only the person who knows the password to access a computer or digital device.

Algorithm Art

Follow the **algorithm** to color in the squares below.

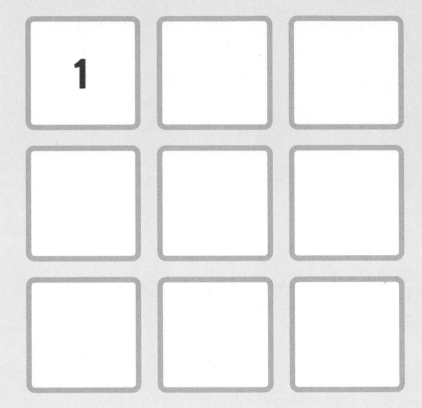

1. Color in square number 1.

2. Move one square right.

3. Move one square right.

4. Color in this square.

5. Move down one square.

6. Move left one square.

7. Color in this square.

8. Move left one square.

9. Move down one square.

10. Color in this square.

11. Move right one square.

12. Move right one square.

13. Color in this square.

14. Look at your pattern!

BRAIN BOX

Algorithms are step-by-step directions that describe how to perform a task. A recipe is an algorithm. We often use a series of steps in math to solve problems quickly—these are also algorithms.

Computers read **algorithms** that are written in code. So can you!

Algorithms

1			

In this code, C means to color a square. An arrow means move one block in the direction of the arrow.

1. Color in square 1.
2. →
3. →
4. →
5. C
6. ↓
7. ←
8. C

9. ←
10. C
11. ←
12. ↓
13. →
14. C
15. →
16. C

17. →
18. ↓
19. C
20. ←
21. ←
22. ←
23. C
[STOP]

Let's Fly!

This drone is ready for liftoff. It can use these commands:

GO FORWARD 1

TURN LEFT

TURN RIGHT

LOOP [GO 1] __ TIMES

Loop commands

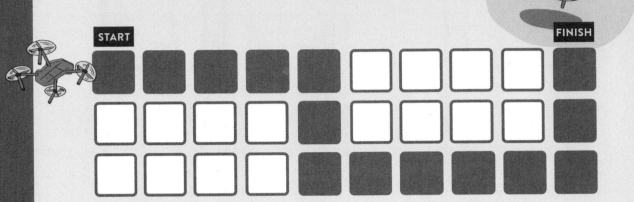

Guide the drone to take the purple path to the landing pad by completing the code.

Loop [Go 1] 5 times

_____

_____

_____

_____

_____

_____

_____

BRAIN BOX

A **loop** is a command that tells the computer to repeat an action. Loops simplify computer programs by grouping repeated commands into a single line of code.

This pilot needs to get to the airport. The plane can use the following commands:

GO FORWARD 1

TURN LEFT

TURN RIGHT

LOOP [GO 1] __ TIMES

Can you write a code that follows the purple path to help the pilot get there?

_____

_____

_____

_____

_____

_____

_____

_____

_____

BRAIN BOX

A **command** is any direction that makes a computer take action.

Cool Conditionals

The penguin wants the fish, but it also wants to avoid the seal. Write a **conditional command** to help the penguin reach the fish.

This command will make the penguin move forward one space:

GO FORWARD 1

If the penguin is going to swim into a seal, you can use a conditional command to change direction:

IF SEAL THEN TURN LEFT

Fill in the commands to get the penguin to follow the purple path to the fish.

Go forward 1

_____

_____

_____

_____

The penguin is still hungry. Can you help the penguin reach more fish?

You can use more than one conditional in a program. Direct the penguin using these commands:

GO FORWARD 1

LOOP [GO 1] _ TIMES

IF SEAL THEN TURN ⬭

IF ORCA THEN TURN ⬭

Fill in the commands to get the penguin along the purple path to the fish.

_____

<u>If seal then turn left</u>

_____

_____

_____

Remember to use a loop command to use fewer Go Forward 1 command blocks.

Screen Time!

Sanjay asks the kids in his class how they use their computers. He makes a graph representing their responses.

Using and analyzing data

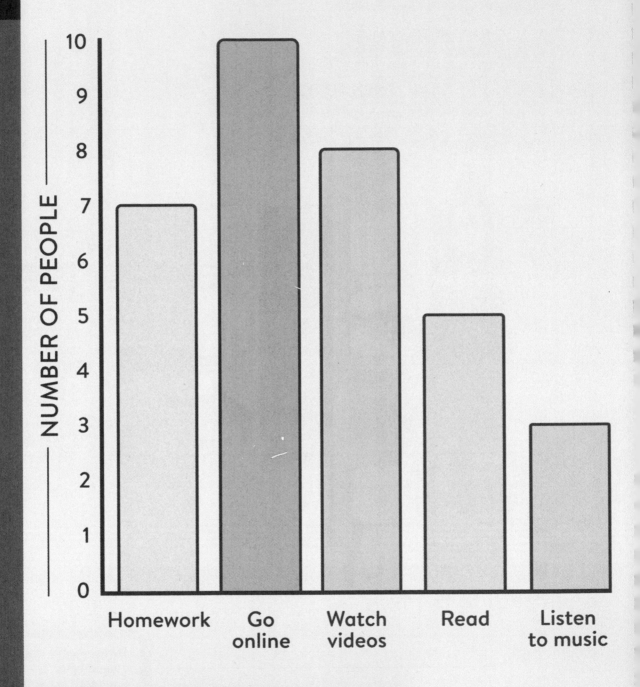

BRAIN BOX

Data is information that people have collected, often to answer a question or solve a problem. Looking at data can help to show other people an idea or predict what might happen in the future. We often use computers to make graphs and help find patterns in data.

Use the graph to answer the questions.

How many people said they used their computer to do homework?

How many more people said they used their computer to go online than to read?

How many fewer people said they use their computer for reading than doing homework?

Which answer did the fewest people choose?

_____

If Sanjay asked another classmate the same question, would they be more likely to pick **go online** or **listen to music**?

_____

How do your friends and family spend their screen time? Fill in the table with their answers!

WAY TO USE THE COMPUTER	NUMBER OF PEOPLE
Homework	
Go online	
Watch videos	
Read	
Listen to music	

Morse Code

Before phones and the internet were invented, people could send messages using **Morse code.**

A •‐	J •‐‐‐	S •••
B ‐•••	K ‐•‐	T ‐
C ‐•‐•	L •‐••	U ••‐
D ‐••	M ‐‐	V •••‐
E •	N ‐•	W •‐‐
F ••‐•	O ‐‐‐	X ‐••‐
G ‐‐•	P •‐‐•	Y ‐•‐‐
H ••••	Q ‐‐•‐	Z ‐‐••
I ••	R •‐•	

What does this message say?

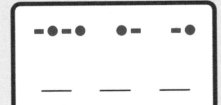

Write your name in Morse code.

BRAIN BOX

In **Morse code,** every letter of the alphabet is made of only two shapes: a dot and a dash. Each letter can be sent by making long and short sounds, or by using long and short flashes of light.

ANSWER KEY

Some problems have only one answer. Some problems have many answers. Turn the page to check your work.

302

SPELLING AND VOCABULARY

pg. 8
stray
cheese
blue
tote
boat
lake
line; rhino
supply
painted; easels
used; key; open; huge
Eight
break

long a words	long e words
stray	cheese
lake	easels
painted	key
eight	
break	

long i words	long o words
line	tote
rhino	boat
supply	open

long u words
blue
huge
studio

pg. 9
friends
ahead
umbrella; bus
bottom; red
laughed; said
grabbed; rink
pig; pink
saddle
bread
wash

short a words	short o words
laughed	bottom
saddle	wash
grabbed	

short e words	short i words
friends	rink
ahead	pig
red	pink
bread	
said	

short u words
umbrella
bus

pg. 10
octopus
coyote
chickens
caterpillar
crabs
hawk
chipmunk
clam; mollusk

pg. 11
night   wrong
write   gnome
autumn   climb
campaign   knowledge
comb   right
raspberry   doubt

pg. 12
swimming   writing
dreaming   running
jumping   digging
asking   changing
driving   winning

pg. 13
wished   nodded
shopped   laughed
lived   smiled
shined   scrubbed
hurried   relied

I am worried about my social studies test tomorrow.
I started sneezing when I smelled the flowers.
The father waved to his daughters as they got on the bus.
Everyone jumped when he popped the balloons.
He started slipping on the icy driveway.
The thief robbed the bank.

pg. 14
weight
receive
thief
sleigh
science
eight
piece
shriek
freight
chief

```
D B K G A S C I E N C E F U
M Y R U O Z L J D R B H R S
S W E I G H T X D C H I E F
V B C M V S H R I E K V I F
P I E C E N I C A L A J G L
O C I G S L E I G H R H R R
H D V K Q U F T B W R H T T
X A E I G H T B O F B R C K
```

pg. 15

Febuary	enuf	shoping	favrit
busy	because	once	hitting
dinasor	suprise	Wensday	receive
peeple	anser	minit	docter
please	calendar	kwite	giving

February; enough; shopping; favorite; dinosaur; surprise; Wednesday; people; answer; minute; doctor; quite

pg. 16
knives   calves
cities   glasses
shelves   brushes
pennies   taxes
witches   candies
turkeys   rays

pg. 17
babies; houses; peaches; foxes; bunnies; boys; puppies; elves; spies; tigers

```
S P I E S Y E Q W J L S
X V O G U E I T M U N Y
P U B A B I E S H O Y X
U L O Q W K N E I B G S
P J Y I C P H L T L P L
P W S O B U N N I E S M
I U K L C P H Q G A D F
E L V E S U Z I E V Z F
S D I Q W B M Y R E R O
M R H O U S E S S B X X
C I K F M C K W V L I E
B V Q M H P E A C H E S
```

pg. 18
children   geese
mice   women
men   oxen
teeth   fish
sheep   moose

pg. 19
preview
misbehaved
rebuild
substandard
misspelled
preheat
repaint

pg. 20
unhappy
unwrap
impatient
impolite
inexpensive
disagree
impossible
dislike
independent

pg. 21
powerful
thoughtful
fearless
hopeful
helpful
colorful
useless
careless

pg. 22

teacher

magician

singer

writer

artist

dancer

actor

violinist

pg. 23
rainy   forgiveness
attractive   repackage
successful   invention
transportation   childlike
reread   buyer
golden   underground
worthless   poisonous

pg. 24
early
day
slow
wet
dull
first
loud
exit
alone
far
on
empty
south
west

pg. 25
hungry = famished
angry = mad
elevated = high
eager = excited
pal = friend
build = construct
wicked = cruel
brag = boast
wealthy = rich
damp = moist

pg. 26
cautious   reckless
sob   laugh
difficult   easy
depart   arrive
exhausted   energetic
repair   break
ill   healthy
complete   begin

alike   different
factual   false

pg. 27
threw   through
their   there
to   two
meet   meat
won   one
write   right
knight   night
fare   fair

pg. 28
creek; creak
aloud; allowed
scent; sent
toad; towed
waist; waste
principal; principle
pair; pear
stationery; stationary

pg. 29
b. very angry
c. worked hard
a. smell
a. climbed up
c. real
c. fancy
c. warned
b. busy

pg. 30
very important
dangerous
amazed
rich
lay back
calm
worn down
easily noticed

pg. 31
1. rabbit; 2. race; 3. rose
1. meat; 2. messy; 3. more
1. mad; 2. map; 3. mouse
1. has; 2. hill; 3. home
1. read; 2. red; 3. ride
1. happy; 2. heavy; 3. hide
1. hall; 2. hello; 3. hero
1. rest; 2. road; 3. rug
1. minus; 2. mitten; 3. money

pg. 33
gift, glow
glow
yes
noun
three

LANGUAGE ARTS

pg. 36
strawberry
eyebrow
wheelbarrow
sidewalk
ponytail
peppermint
butterfly
playground

```
H W K J W P O N Y T A I L F A
A H B G B L V I P F C E L B Z
B E S T R A W B E R R Y E P D
U E D L T Y L M P J M E D I O
T L F A H G E H P L C B E R A
T B I B R A C E B O R R B G J
E A N B U O D K R F E O N J V
R R J P D U V J M P O W G U N
F R G A K N K S I D E W A L K
L O Q M S D O Q N H S I V S R
Y W K C H K M D T H T Y B T F
F A D L Q R K J O B B L A I C
```

pg. 37
hallway; bedroom
necktie
everyone; basketball
jellyfish

turtleneck; wintertime
starfish
fishbowl; goldfish
snowfall; snowman
(Answers may vary)
hall + way = hallway
bed + room = bedroom
neck + tie = necktie

pg. 38

black, green, purple, yellow, orange
monkey, rhino, panda, gorilla, kangaroo
brain, lungs, heart, blood, bones

pg. 39

where
watch
shall
bead
beard
are
gone
mood
now
foot
although

pg. 40

two-syllable words:
spelling
question
ladder
birthday
three-syllable words:
dinosaur
bumblebee
accident
grandmother
four-syllable words:
operator
biography
adorable
caterpillar

pg. 41

cloak; croak; crook; brook; broom
blond; blood; flood; floor; flour

pg. 42

string
green
day
patient
girl
pounds
food
water

pg. 44

couldn't = could not
she's = she is
didn't = did not
they're = they are
what's = what is
weren't = were not
don't = do not
we'll = we will
he'd = he would / he had
it's = it is

pg. 45

I'm, I've, he's, We've, They're, weren't, couldn't, I'll, what's

pg. 46

feather
desert
ice
mouse
skyscraper
ghost
elephant

pg. 48–49

(Some answers will vary)
told all/confessed
is reading
help me
listening
made me scared
easy
joking with me
two of a kind
makes me crazy

pg. 50

A Trip to the Wetland
by Elissa
Today, our class took a trip to a local wetland with our teacher, Ms. Casamo. The tour guide, Ranger Sala, walked us around. In a wetland, she said, water covers the land, and plants grow in wet soil. Here, many animals such as frogs, salamanders, snakes, and birds make their home. Ranger Sala asked if anyone could name a wetland. Antonio asked whether Everglades National Park, in Florida, is a wetland.
"It is!" Sala said. "And did you know that it is the only spot on Earth where both alligators and crocodiles live together?"
Before we left, I saw a bird called a great blue heron standing in the water. It was so still, I thought it might be a statue!

pg. 51

Proper nouns: Ms. Ramos, January, Penny, Maple Street, Grand Canyon, Arizona, Dylan, Aunt Ethel, Sugar Shack, Dr. Pollock, Sunday, Labor Day
Common nouns: class, zoo, house, shoelaces, shoes, doughnuts, family, beach, pool

pg. 52

an; the; an
the; the; a
the; a; the
an; the; the

pg. 53

The dinosaur skeleton in the museum was so tall it almost touched the ceiling.
Nana said she would take me to school today.
Plants need light, water, and nutrient-rich soil so they can grow.
Lucas said he was practicing for the spelling bee every day.
Everyone should bring their pencils to class tomorrow.
Cora and I were so excited to see the parade, we arrived an hour early.
I didn't see the person who returned the book to me. They left it on my desk before school.
Squirrels bury nuts so they can eat in the winter.
The teacher said students should contact them with any questions.
The class that raised the most money for the animal shelter was ours!

pg. 54

his/theirs; his/their
mine; my
his; his
ours; Our

pg. 55

your; yours
hers; her
theirs; their
its

pg. 56

My teacher's reading contest is going to start next week.
I didn't realize that was Sari's house.
Samantha's cupcakes were absolutely delicious!
My friend's Halloween party was a little spooky.
Did you know that this is Lalo's trumpet?
I promised I would clean out my dad's car.
Kody's sister won the spelling bee.

pg. 57

friends'
teacher's
tree's
Molly's
girl's
giraffes'
teachers'
bulls'
travelers'
girls'

pg. 58

three; enormous; sweet-smelling
two; delicious; meatless
five; spicy; roasted
tiny; brown; loud
large; blue
noisy; timpani
quiet; gray
Taste or smell: sweet-smelling, delicious, spicy
Color: brown, blue, gray
Number: three, two, five
Size: enormous, tiny, large
Kind: meatless, roasted, timpani
Sound: loud, noisy, quiet

pg. 60

rougher
hungriest
fastest
shorter
slowest
brightest
gooder = better
farest = farthest
badder = worse

pg. 61

bowls
figure
works
investigate
dresses
prepares
dance
read

pg. 62

will go = future
eats = present
cooked = past
sings = present
hunted = past
lived = past
walks = present
will ride = future
will plant = future

pg. 64

Action verbs: play, hits, pitches, slams, walks, shouts, hurts, slides, examines, tapes, catches, win
Scramble:
slams   win
slides   pitches
walks   play
examines   catches
hits   hurts
shouts   tapes

pg. 65

were
was
are

is
have
am
would
has
could

pg. 66

is
was
am
are
feels
seems
looks
smells

pg. 67

Across	Down
read	drank
gave	caught
threw	wrote
rang	bought
brought	hid

```
D   C
R E A D
A   U
N   G A V E          B
K   H          B R O U G H T
    T H R E W  U     I
    R A N G    G     D
    O          H
    T          T
    E
```

pg. 68

Present-tense verbs: am, get, is, eat, spend, eat, go, choose, sing, spend, play, wear, give, promise
Yesterday I went to soccer camp.
When I got there, I caught up with my camp friends before dinner.
I ate breakfast in the mess hall and then spent the morning practicing drills.
After activities we spent more time playing soccer.
On the last night of camp, we all played a joke on our coaches and wore our pajamas to the game.

pg. 69

Shai plays soccer outside.
Samuel played the computer game skillfully.
Did it rain today?
There are mosquitoes everywhere.
The ballerina danced gracefully.
The boys waited patiently for their turn.
Kiko walked upstairs.
The rock star played his guitar yesterday.
Tomorrow, I will eat a burrito for lunch.
how: skillfully, gracefully, patiently
when: today, yesterday, tomorrow
where: outside, everywhere, upstairs

pg. 70

The funny clown rode on a tiny bike.
The sandy beach was very crowded.
The mothers took their children to the park.
All of the dogs began to bark.
The Peterson family is going to the mountains tomorrow.

The grumpy man yelled at the noisy boys.
Christian likes to visit his grandparents.
Dawn won a ribbon at the horse show.

pg. 73

My horse won its first race today.
I hope it's ready. I'm really hungry!
You should buy that sweater. Its color is perfect for you.
The elephant and its new baby can now be seen at the zoo.
It's time to leave for the movies.
That's a cute puppy. What is its name?
I wonder if it's hot outside today.
Hurry up! It's going to rain soon.
What a pretty bird. Its feathers are a beautiful color.
Have you seen my book? It's not in its usual place on my desk.

pg. 74

Please put the flowers there.
Have you been there before?
They're going to the zoo tomorrow.
Have you seen their new car?
I like swimming in pools when they're not too crowded.
Your pencil is over there on the desk.
Their house is right next to ours.
Will you go there with me?
On Saturday, they're having a birthday party.
I just saw their new lizard.

pg. 75

I don't know where we are going on vacation.
If we're late, he won't let us in.
What were you buying in that store?
Tomorrow, we're going to canoe on the lake.
Do you remember where Kelly said we should meet her?
We were in Florida last winter.
We're not singing in the school concert this year.
Where is your new bicycle?
Do you remember where you left your coat?
They were the winning team in the relay race.

pg. 76

wave
tie
watch
row
spring
letter
bat

pg. 77

Kevin said, "Let's go to the zoo tomorrow."
"Is that your new dress?" asked Chitra.
"Here we are at last!" said Ari. "I can't wait to see this movie!"
"I'm cooking spaghetti for dinner," said Rudi's father.
David asked, "Why are you laughing so hard?"
"There was one third grader," said the teacher, "who got every answer right."
"You'd better wear your coat. It's very cold today," said Philip's grandfather.
"I'm having my birthday party at the bowling alley," said Carlo.
"Are you going to play soccer this year?" asked Li.
"Watch out! There's a car coming!" yelled Alan.

pg. 78

My new dog has one black ear.
What time is your piano lesson?
Where did you put your boots?
That is so exciting!
Julia and Jeffrey both live in North Carolina.
Hurry, the bathtub is overflowing onto the floor!
Oh no, our dinner is burning!
How long will you be gone?
That is so wonderful! OR That is so wonderful.

pg. 79

January 14, 2023
Dear Hernando,
    I am so excited. We are now in our new home in Middletown, Pennsylvania. Our kitchen has a new stove, refrigerator, microwave, and sink. I have my own bedroom with a nice view.
    Middletown is a lot smaller than Philadelphia, Pennsylvania, where we used to live. It is so different from living in a smaller town.
    I can't wait to see you at camp this summer. We'll sail boats, go horseback riding, swim, and play tennis. I hope we'll be in the same tent like we were last year!
Your friend,
Neel

Neel McFadden
1234 Main Street
Middletown, PA 10001

Hernando Green
9876 1st Street
Philadelphia, PA 19100

pg. 80

I watched the Red Sox play against the Yankees last night.
Sashiko lives in the United States, but she was born in Japan.
Is your Uncle Fred coming to your house for Thanksgiving?
We swam in the Pacific Ocean on our vacation last year.
I can't wait for school to start in September.
Can you help me find Ms. Heather?
Chris was born in Dallas.
We are going to Disneyland on Friday.
Person:
I, Sashiko, Uncle Fred, We, Ms. Heather, Chris
Place:
United States, Japan, Pacific Ocean, Dallas, Disneyland
Thing:
Red Sox, Yankees, Thanksgiving, September, Friday

READING

pg. 83

Effect:
- Coyote decided to go for a walk.
- A cloud appeared in the sky.
- It began to sprinkle.
- The creek turned into a large, swirling river.

Cause:
- Coyote wanted more rain.
- Coyote wished he could cool his feet.

pg. 85

(Some answers will vary)
- Around the year 1508 BCE
- the foremost of noble ladies

- the supreme ruler of ancient Egypt
- Neferure
- Hatsheput's husband Tuthmosis II died, which meant that her stepson became pharaoh. But her stepson was only three years old and too young to lead. So, Hetseheput became his coruler.
- directed the building of monuments, organized trade networks, organized an expedition down the east coast of Africa
- more than twenty years

pg. 87

- Life on the pond is boring.
- The duck wishes it could hop.
- The duck wants to ride on the kangaroo's back.
- The kangaroo tells the duck to sit on the end of its tail.

pg. 89

c; d; c; how to plant and care for the seeds, how to make tools, how to live with the creatures

pg. 91

(Some answers will vary)
- to see if the heat from his body would hatch the eggs
- He sold newspapers, food, and candy.
- the sole right given to an inventor to make or sell his idea
- because no one wanted it
- success takes a lot of hard work

pg. 93

- 4
- baking powder
- before
- yes, when both sides are brown
- flour, sugar, salt, baking powder
- milk, eggs, melted butter, vanilla
- about one minute
- warm and with syrup

pg. 95

(Some answers will vary)
- loving, poor, kind
- a loaf of bread, a few eggs, and a cabbage
- because when they opened their cupboards they were suddenly filled with all sorts of delicious foods and fresh juices; also, their clothes turned into robes of fine linen and their hovel turned into a great palace
- because they loved each other
- to never have to live without the other
- they are different trees but grew from the same trunk

pg. 97

(Some answers will vary)
- It is difficult to please everyone.

pg. 99

(Some answers will vary) • c
- because whoever pulls it free will become the new king of Britain
- because he is a young boy
- c
- surprised, because he did not expect to become king

pg. 101

5
4
2
3
1

pg. 103

(Some answers will vary)
- c
- make him a suit of the finest cloth imaginable
- because they did not want him to think that they were not smart enough to appreciate the cloth
- c
- His vanity caused him more harm than good.

pg. 105

- because it contains a lot of iron oxide in its soil
- dry and cold
- Olympus Mons
- two: Phobos and Deimos
- 687 Earth days
- orbiters, landers, rovers
- clues that life may have existed billions of years ago

pg. 106

b; c; c

WRITING

pg. 114

pool; I will
When I go to the pool, I will swim and dive off the diving board.
everyone was
Everyone was excited and having fun.
the boys
The boys put on their uniforms and ran out onto the baseball field.
the fans
The fans were really excited at the soccer game and cheered loudly for their team.

pg. 116

(Some answers will vary)
- Many animals can produce their own light.
- Today, we started our schoolwide recycling challenge.
- There are some essential items you should bring on a camping trip.

pg. 118

Katie had a great time at tennis practice this morning. First she practiced her forehand shot with her coach. Then she worked on her backhand with the ball machine. Once she was warmed up, Katie and her coach played a few practice games, so she could work on her serve. Katie was exhausted when she got home, but at least she felt ready for Saturday's tournament.

pg. 119

Green card	Yellow card
2	4
1	2
3	3
4	1

Purple card
2
3
1
4

pg. 122

(Answers may vary)
- running is the ideal type of exercise
- opinion
- running is something almost anyone can do; running burns calories and

gives your heart and legs a great workout; running is something you can do with a friend or by yourself

pg. 125
I. c. How Halloween started
II. b. Making a costume
III. b. Making a jack-o'-lantern
IV. b. Knocking on doors

pg. 131
If you travel to hawai'i, don't forget to visit the Mauna Loa Volcano. Mauna Loa is the the biggest Volcano on earth, and one of the most active Tourists visit from all over the World to see hot, red lava flowing from the volcano down into the Pacific Ocean below.

Mauna Loa is located on the the island of Hawai'i, and it is part of Hawai'i Volcanoes National park. The park is so big that it could take you several days just to drive arund and see all the sights. ¶Be sure to pack your raincoat and boots, because it's often cool and cloudy rainy at the top of the volcano. Of course, as soon as you drive down to sea level, the weather gets warmer and sunnier, that's Hawai'i!

MATH SKILLS

pg. 134
Even: 4, 2, 12, 146, 28, 70, 34, 18, 164, 500, 998, 744
Odd: 9, 17, 99, 239, 501, 23, 39, 301, 55, 87, 101, 219, 989, 3, 25
Even: 8, 10, 12, 14, 16, 18
Odd: 9, 11, 13, 15, 17
even
even
odd

pg. 135
10   12   25
15   36   25
100   333

pg. 136
hundreds   5
thousands   2
70,208

pg. 137
hundreds   277,539
2   75,222
thousands   4,601
3
Forty-eight thousand, five hundred, sixty seven

pg. 138
2   70   8000
160   4   6
3   5   103

pg. 139
ray
line
ray
line segment

pg. 140
acute   right   obtuse
   right   obtuse
   obtuse   acute

pg. 141
3   8
4   right

pg. 142
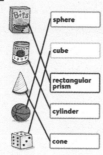

pg. 143
square; circle; 6; triangle; because it isn't 3D; none; cube; 2; circle; cylinder; sphere

pg. 144

o, P
n, m
s, u
h, s

pg. 145
77; 88
44,444; 444,444
42; 49
150; 175
7; 6
23; 30
12; 16

pg. 146
60	10	30	80
60	40	40	80
20	70	20	20
800	500	700	600
900	300	700	400
300	200	100	200
400	900	900	200

pg. 147
60,000
29,000
40,000
40,000
4,000

pg. 148
80 + 20 = 100
60 + 70 = 130
90 – 30 = 60
100 – 70 = 30
60 + 20 = 80
40 + 30 = 70
90 + 10 = 100
40 + 30 = 70
70 – 10 = 60
70 – 30 = 40
50 – 40 = 10
90 – 40 = 50

pg. 149
900 + 200 = 1100
900 + 600 = 1500
700 + 200 = 900
600 + 300 = 900
300 + 200 = 500
700 + 300 = 1000
700 + 500 = 1200
500 + 400 = 900
400 + 100 = 500
800 + 800 = 1600
900 + 600 = 1500
700 + 200 = 900

pg. 150
May; 30; June; 5; 70

pg. 151
8; dog; snake; 2; hamsters; 6

pg. 152
17; 31; 15; diving; high and low jumps; 10; diving events

pg. 153
(10) × 4 = 40
27 ÷ (9) = 3   (5) × (7) = 35
(28) ÷ 4 = 7   (3) – 3 = 0
8 + (7) = 15   (6) + (3) = 9
4 + (56) = 60

ADDITION AND SUBTRACTION

pg. 156
2 + 9 = 11
9 + 2 = 11
11 – 2 = 9
11 – 9 = 2

7 + 8 = 15
8 + 7 = 15
15 – 7 = 8
15 – 8 = 7

8 + 9 = 17
9 + 8 = 17
17 – 8 = 9
17 – 9 = 8

5 + 8 = 13
8 + 5 = 13
13 – 5 = 8
13 – 8 = 5

5 + 14 = 19
14 + 5 = 19
19 – 5 = 14
19 – 14 = 5

3 + 7 = 10
7 + 3 = 10
10 – 3 = 7
10 – 7 = 3

pg. 157
6 + 8 = 14
8 + 6 = 14
14 – 6 = 8
14 – 8 = 6

6 + 7 = 13
7 + 6 = 13
13 – 6 = 7
13 – 7 = 6

5 + 6 = 11
6 + 5 = 11
11 – 5 = 6
11 – 6 = 5

2 + 6 = 8
6 + 2 = 8
8 – 2 = 6
8 – 6 = 2

5 + 7 = 12
7 + 5 = 12
12 – 5 = 7
12 – 7 = 5

5 + 15 = 20
15 + 5 = 20
20 – 5 = 15
20 – 15 = 5

6 + 11 = 17
11 + 6 = 17
17 – 6 = 11
17 – 11 = 6

pg. 158
49	777	98	799
99	949	898	78
88	867	999	978

pg. 159
26   29   26   30
27; 26; 41; 32; 30; 35; 36

pg. 160
36	452	43	756
23	471	255	13
37	142	889	342

pg. 161
16 – 8 = 8   24 – 10 = 14
24 + 35 = 59   35 – 15 = 20
41 + 15 = 56   21 + 15 = 36
22 + 62 = 84   22 + 63 = 85

pg. 162
4	3	8
9	5	1
2	7	6

8	13	6
7	9	11
12	5	10

10	3	8
5	7	9
6	11	4

pg. 163
13	8	9
6	10	14
11	12	7

7	6	11
12	8	4
5	10	9

16	3	2	13
5	10	11	8
9	6	7	12
4	15	14	1

14	9	13	2
3	12	8	15
4	11	7	16
17	6	10	5

pg. 164
41   82   65
630   651   744
507   842   943

pg. 165
453   671   923
706   926   229
494   663   620
838   550   948

pg. 166
28   38   19
259   569   348
579   348   357

pg. 167
116   380   599
289   421   324
473   473   666

pg. 168
836   488   727
227   536   557
657   727   338

pg. 169
169   813   367
132   555   227
164   768   443

pg. 170
9 + 11 = 20
11 – 5 = 6
3 + 6 = 9
125 – 75 = 50
37 – 2 = 35
68 + 12 = 80
12 + 12 – 24 = 0
150 – 100 + 14 = 64

305

306

22 − 12 + 11 = 21
21 + 33 + 3 = 57
33 + 11 − 10 = 34
47 − 15 − 3 = 29

pg. 171

388	523	977
890	378	812
545	1,079	589
825	766	896
454	524	499

pg. 172

645 211 472
443 611 782 636
324 440 642
541 701 712
685 41

MULTIPLICATION and DIVISION

pg. 174

6 7 5 8
0 3 2 1
4 4 9 2
10 6 5 7
1 2 3 4 5 6 7 8 9 10

pg. 175

2 6 12 14
10 8 10 16
20 4 18 12
6 8 18 0
2 4 6 8 10 12 14 16 18 20

pg. 176

3 21 0 12
30 9 18 6
27 15 21 15
12 24 18 30
3 6 9 12 15 18 21 24 27 30

pg. 177

8 32 24 12
20 40
36 4
28 8 36 24
12 16 20 0
4 8 12 16 20 24 28 32 36 40

pg. 178

20 25 10 35
45 0 50 40
5 10 45 30
15 20 40 15
5 10 15 20 25 30 35 40 45 50

pg. 179

12 0 30 42
18 24 12 48
54 36 30 18
60 24 54 6
6 12 18 24 30 36 42 48 54 60

pg. 180

42 7 35 49
21 28 56 0
7 63 14 70
35 28 63 56
7 14 21 28 35 42 49 56 63 70

pg. 181

56 48 32 80
40 56 0 24
72 16 64 16
48 40 80 56
8 16 24 32 40 48 56 64 72 80

pg. 182

9 63 45 81
27 54 18 0
54 36 72 90
45 72 63 36
9 18 27 36 45 54 63 72 81 90

pg. 183

36 27
72 81
54 9
18 63
45 90

pg. 184

10 40 80
70 90 60
50 100 40
30 20 70
10 20 30 40 50 60 70 80 90 100

pg. 185

1 4 9 16
25 36 49 64
81 100 121 144
11 22 33 44 55 66 77 88 99 110
12 24 36 48 60 72 84 96 108 120

pg. 186

36 36 24 24
56 56 14 14
20 20 30 30
728,540

pg. 187

4 8 12 16 20 24 28 32 36 40
5 10 15 20 25 30 35 40 45 50
6 12 18 24 30 36 42 48 54 60
7 14 21 28 35 42 49 56 63 70
8 16 24 32 40 48 56 64 72 80

pg. 188

2 × 4 = 8   1 × 10 = 10
6 × 7 = 42   4 × 8 = 32
8 × 8 = 64   2 × 6 = 12
5 × 7 = 35   7 × 7 = 49
4 × 9 = 36   8 × 9 = 72
6 × 8 = 48   6 × 3 = 18
3 × 7 = 21   5 × 2 = 10
9 × 0 = 0   6 × 9 = 54
4 × 7 = 28   9 × 3 = 27

pg. 189

×	0	1	2	3	4	5	6	7	8	9	10	11	12
0	0	0	0	0	0	0	0	0	0	0	0	0	0
1	0	1	2	3	4	5	6	7	8	9	10	11	12
2	0	2	4	6	8	10	12	14	16	18	20	22	24
3	0	3	6	9	12	15	18	21	24	27	30	33	36
4	0	4	8	12	16	20	24	28	32	36	40	44	48
5	0	5	10	15	20	25	30	35	40	45	50	55	60
6	0	6	12	18	24	30	36	42	48	54	60	66	72
7	0	7	14	21	28	35	42	49	56	63	70	77	84
8	0	8	16	24	32	40	48	56	64	72	80	88	96
9	0	9	18	27	36	45	54	63	72	81	90	99	108
10	0	10	20	30	40	50	60	70	80	90	100	110	120
11	0	11	22	33	44	55	66	77	88	99	110	121	132
12	0	12	24	36	48	60	72	84	96	108	120	132	144

pg. 190

28 186 155 208
84 720 488 219
98 88 156 540

pg. 191

207 288 312
225 574 78
416 594 595
564 185 384

pg. 192

8 3
3 3

pg. 193

4 2 6 5
2 10 2 11
4 3 4 6

8 7 2 9
1 9 9 10

pg. 194

18 ÷ 2 = 9
12 ÷ 3 = 4
48 ÷ 4 = 12
12 ÷ 2 = 6
12 ÷ 3 = 4

pg. 195

20 ÷ 4 = 5
30 ÷ 5 = 6
88 ÷ 11 = 8
56 ÷ 8 = 7
18 ÷ 3 = 6

pg. 196

12	4 × 3 = 12
3	3 × 4 = 12
4	12 ÷ 3 = 4
	12 ÷ 4 = 3

32	4 × 8 = 32
8	8 × 4 = 32
4	32 ÷ 4 = 8
	32 ÷ 8 = 4

35	5 × 7 = 35
7	7 × 5 = 35
5	35 ÷ 5 = 7
	35 ÷ 7 = 5

28	4 × 7 = 28
7	7 × 4 = 28
4	28 ÷ 4 = 7
	28 ÷ 7 = 4

45	5 × 9 = 45
9	9 × 5 = 45
5	45 ÷ 5 = 9
	45 ÷ 9 = 5

pg. 197

9	9 × 2 = 18
2	2 × 9 = 18
18	18 ÷ 2 = 9
	18 ÷ 9 = 2

6	6 × 5 = 30
5	5 × 6 = 30
30	30 ÷ 6 = 5
	30 ÷ 5 = 6

6	6 × 2 = 12
2	2 × 6 = 12
12	12 ÷ 6 = 2
	12 ÷ 2 = 6

9	9 × 8 = 72
8	8 × 9 = 72
72	72 ÷ 9 = 8
	72 ÷ 8 = 9

48	8 × 6 = 48
6	6 × 8 = 48
	48 ÷ 6 = 8
	48 ÷ 8 = 6

7	7 × 8 = 56
8	8 × 7 = 56
56	56 ÷ 7 = 8
	56 ÷ 8 = 7

40	8 × 5 = 40
5	5 × 8 = 40
8	40 ÷ 5 = 8
	40 ÷ 8 = 5

9	9 × 7 = 63
7	7 × 9 = 63
63	63 ÷ 9 = 7
	63 ÷ 7 = 9

pg. 198

8 ÷ 8 = 1
8 × 8 = 64   18 ÷ 9 = 2   6 × 5 = 30
7 × 9 = 63   7 × 2 = 14   64 ÷ 8 = 8
32 ÷ 4 = 8   27 ÷ 3 = 9   8 ÷ 2 = 4
9 × 5 = 45   6 × 8 = 48   12 ÷ 3 = 4
6 ÷ 3 = 2   9 ÷ 3 = 3   3 × 7 = 21
                                49 ÷ 7 = 7
                                2 × 4 = 8
                                56 ÷ 7 = 8

pg. 199

27 36 7 28
4 4 49 63
54 4 24 5
36 27 42 3
195 25 16 9

pg. 200

24
27
3
120 seconds
2 minutes

FRACTIONS and DECIMALS

pg. 202

4   6

3   2

$\frac{3}{4}$ $\frac{2}{6}$

pg. 203

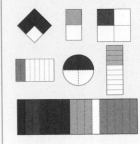

8   8
6   4
$\frac{6}{8}$ $\frac{4}{8}$

pg. 204

$\frac{1}{4}$ $\frac{2}{3}$ $\frac{2}{4}$
$\frac{1}{3}$ $\frac{7}{10}$ $\frac{4}{8}$

pg. 205

(Some answers will vary)

$\frac{1}{16}$

pg. 206

$\frac{3}{10}$
$\frac{4}{10}$ $\frac{3}{10}$
$\frac{1}{10}$ $\frac{6}{10}$

pg. 207

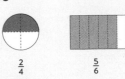

$\frac{1}{3}$

$\frac{1}{5}$

$\frac{1}{4}$

pg. 208

20 ÷ 4 = 5 $\frac{1}{4}$ of 20 = 5
6 ÷ 2 = 3 $\frac{1}{2}$ of 6 = 3
10 ÷ 5 = 2 $\frac{1}{5}$ of 10 = 2
8 ÷ 2 = 4 $\frac{1}{2}$ of 8 = 4

pg. 209

4 ÷ 2 = 2 $\frac{1}{2}$ of 4 = 2
15 ÷ 3 = 5 $\frac{1}{3}$ of 15 = 5
16 ÷ 2 = 8 $\frac{1}{2}$ of 16 = 8
15 ÷ 5 = 3 $\frac{1}{5}$ of 15 = 3
12 ÷ 6 = 2 $\frac{1}{6}$ of 12 = 2

pg. 210

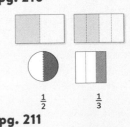

$\frac{1}{2}$ $\frac{1}{3}$

pg. 211

$\frac{2}{4}$ $\frac{5}{6}$

$\frac{4}{9}$

pg. 212

$\frac{2}{3}$ $\frac{4}{5}$

$\frac{4}{4}$ $\frac{3}{4}$

$\frac{9}{10}$ $\frac{4}{6}$

$\frac{9}{12}$ $\frac{7}{8}$

$\frac{2}{5}$

$\frac{2}{4}$

pg. 213

$\frac{4}{6}$ $\frac{2}{5}$

$\frac{4}{7}$ $\frac{2}{4}$

$\frac{7}{12}$ $\frac{2}{8}$

$\frac{3}{10}$ $\frac{4}{9}$

$\frac{3}{5}$

$\frac{3}{6}$

pg. 214

$\frac{2}{3}$ $\frac{8}{10}$

$\frac{1}{6}$ $\frac{5}{7}$

$21 \div 3 = 7$ 7

$16 \div 8 = 2$ 2

$18 \div 2 = 9$ 9

$20 \div 10 = 2$ 2

$24 \div 4 = 6$ 6

pg. 215

$\frac{3}{10}$ $\frac{5}{8}$

$\frac{7}{7} + \frac{7}{7} = 2$

$\frac{6}{6} = 1$

$\frac{1}{2} + \frac{1}{2} = \frac{2}{2}$

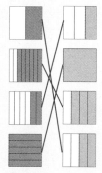

pg. 216

$\frac{4}{10} = .4$ $\frac{2}{10} = .2$ $\frac{5}{10} = .5$

$\frac{8}{10} = .8$

$\frac{9}{10} = .9$ $\frac{1}{10} = .1$ $\frac{4}{10} = .4$

$\frac{2}{10} = .2$ $\frac{5}{10} = .5$ $\frac{7}{10} = .7$

$.6 = \frac{6}{10}$ $.8 = \frac{8}{10}$ $.1 = \frac{1}{10}$

pg. 217

$\frac{8}{100} = 0.08$

$\frac{3}{100} = 0.03$ $\frac{2}{100} = 0.02$

$\frac{5}{100} = 0.05$ $\frac{9}{100} = 0.09$

$\frac{8}{100} = 0.08$ $\frac{6}{100} = 0.06$

$0.09 = \frac{9}{100}$ $0.01 = \frac{1}{100}$ $0.04 = \frac{4}{100}$

pg. 218

tenths; 7; 1; Ones

pg. 219

thousandths; 85.341; 2; 32.479; 3.01; 40.001

pg. 220

6.8   13.9   6.5
10.47   12.87   7.96
8.07   8.55   10.94
11.60   11.57   9.49

pg. 221

3.2   2.2   .36
4.45   5.13   2.59
5.19   4.94   3.26
4.04   4.81   1.82

pg. 222

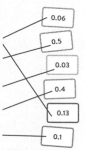

0.06
0.5
0.03
0.4
0.13
0.1

MEASUREMENT

pg. 224

inches; miles; feet;
3 inches; 15 feet; 7 yards;
7 feet; 100 yards

pg. 225

20 inches < 2 feet
2 yards = 72 inches
6 feet < 3 yards
10 feet = 120 inches
1 mile > 5,000 feet
36; 30; 1; 12; 4; 10,560

pg. 226

centimeter; kilometer; meter;
41 kilometers; 2 meters;
3 centimeters; 1 ½ meters

pg. 227

6 inches   15.3 centimeters
1.2 inch   3.2 centimeters
2.7 inches 7.4 centimeters

pg. 228

4 cups; 16 quarts; 2 cups; 8 pints

pg. 229

ounces; pounds; ounces; pounds;
tons; pounds; tons

pg. 230

8; 8
16; 4; 10
6; 15; 9

pg. 231

6; 4;
4 (width) × 6 (length);
24 square units;
12; 20; 24;
28 square feet

pg. 232

6 + 6 + 6 = 18 ft
3 + 3 + 3 + 3 + 3 + 3 + 3 + 3 = 24 in
5 + 5 + 5 + 5 = 20 in
10 + 10 + 4 + 4 = 28 in

TIME AND MONEY

pg. 234

6:00   8:35   2:15   2:45
        3:55   5:45   9:40
        10:05   5:25   12:00
        7:25   2:00   3:30

pg. 235

6:40
7:30
Rick; 24; 90; 90

pg. 236

1 ½ hours; 5:00 p.m; 8:20 p.m;
45 minutes; 2:30 p.m; 1 hour,
15 minutes

pg. 237

1 hour, 45 minutes; 1 hour, 55
minutes; 10:45 a.m; 4:55 p.m;
3:15 p.m.

pg. 238

$.35; $1.05; $1.25; Laura; $1.25;
Allison

pg. 239

$1.05; $1.09; $.59; $1.23

pg. 240

$3.69 $3.42 $1.60
$3.10 $1.00 $12.98
$12.00 $5.20 $9.81
$1.41 $9.27 $.62
$2.87 $.02 $8.67

pg. 241

$3.00
$.20
$3.20
$2.00
no

pg. 242

$.05 $.71 $.01
$.53 $.75 $3.65
$4.03 $1.00 $.37

WORD PROBLEMS

pg. 244

45 + 36 = 81
15 + 9 = 24
45 + 20 = 65
10 + 12 + 8 + 6 = 36

pg. 245

55 + 19 + 31 = 105
10 + 15 + 18 + 20 = 63

pg. 246

47 − 35 = 12
(88 − 26) − 41 = 21
85 − 72 = 13
38 − (9 + 10 + 2) = 17

pg. 247

100 − 86 = 14
375 − 320 = 55
$130 − $75 = $55

pg. 248

55 ÷ 5 = 11
81 ÷ 9 = 9
24 ÷ 8 = 3
56 ÷ 8 = 7

pg. 249

50 x 4 = 200
9 x 6 = 54
12 x 2 = 24
42 x 5 = 210

pg. 250

87 − 65 = 22; subtraction
9 x 5 = 45; multiplication
26 + 34 = 60; addition
72 ÷ 9 = 8; division

pg. 251

64 − 46 = 18
20 x 4 = 80
12 + 4 = 16
$25 + $25 = $50

pg. 252

5 crayons + 4 index cards + 3
markers + 2 glue sticks + 1 pair of
scissors = 15 items,
20 items total − 15 items = 5 pencils
10 ÷ 2 = 5, 18 − 5 = 13
3 + 3 + 3 = 9, 10 x 9 = 90
64 ÷ 4 = 16, 36 ÷ 4 = 9, 16 + 9 = 25

SOCIAL STUDIES

pg. 255

Ohio
Michigan
Illinois
Kentucky
Missouri
Minnesota, Wisconsin, Illinois,
Missouri, Nebraska, and South Dakota
Maine
Montana
Utah, Colorado, Arizona, and
New Mexico
Kansas
Two; North Carolina, North Dakota
One; West Virginia

pg. 256

Alaska, Texas
Rhode Island, Delaware
New Hampshire, Vermont
false (west and southwest regions)
Hawai'i

pg. 257

[column 1]
Texas
Washington
Pennsylvania
Missouri
[column 2]
Massachusetts
Wisconsin
Ohio
Maryland
[column 3]
Georgia
Illinois
California
Pennsylvania

pg. 260

AL   CO
AK   CT
AZ   DE
AR   FL
CA   GA

pg. 261

HI   MO   RI
ID   MT   SC
IL   NE   SD
IN   NV   TN
IA   NH   TX
KS   NJ   UT
KY   NM   VT
LA   NY   VA
ME   NC   WA
MD   ND   WV
MA   OH   WI
MI   OK   WY
MN   OR
MS   PA
Washington, DC
District of Columbia

308

pg. 263

- A set of laws that states the rights of US citizens, and describes US government.
- a democracy
- They are elected by the people through voting.
- White men participated in democracy because they were allowed to vote. Women of all races, Black men, and Indigenous men were excluded.
- Freedom of speech, freedom of religion, freedom of the press and/ or the right to a fair trial.

pg. 265

- Executive, legislative, judicial
- So that there is a system of checks and balances
- The president
- The Senate and the House of Representatives
- 100; 2
- The Supreme Court
- Smaller states have lower populations.

pg. 266

1851
Montana
before

pg. 267

No, because there were laws that prevented women of color from freely exercising their right to vote until 1962.
The Voting Rights Act of 1965 outlawed discriminatory voting practices and allowed people of color to exercise their right to vote.

pg. 268

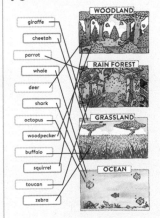

SCIENCE

pg. 271

(Some answers may vary)
chapter 2
p. 3
chapter 3
p. 40
table of contents
index
glossary

pg. 273

1. egg   2. pupa
3. caterpillar   4. adult
Lepidoptera: a group of insects
migrate: make a journey to a new place

moths
– have plump, furry bodies
– have a dull color
– fly at night
– have a plain or feathery antennae
– rest with their wings stretched out flat

both
– belong to *Lepidoptera* group
– have six legs
– scales cover wings
– 2 pairs of wings
– 4 stages of development

butterflies
– have slender, hairless bodies
– are brightly colored
– fly during the day
– their antennae are knobbed at the tips
– hold their wings upright while they are resting

pg. 275

(sample answers)
mammals: people, dogs, mice
birds: hawks, barn owls, toucans
amphibians: salamanders, frogs, toads
reptiles: geckos, crocodiles, boa constrictors
fish: goldfish, sharks, eels

	mammals	birds	amphibians	reptiles	fish
warm-blooded	✓	✓			
cold-blooded			✓	✓	✓

pg. 276

Penguins, ostriches
Migration
They have no teeth!
Hawks, eagles, owls

pg. 277

1. Their huge eyes can see well in the dark.
2. Their hearing is very sensitive.
3. Soft-fringed feathers on their wings help them fly quickly.
4. They have needle-sharp claws called talons.
They are spit up in pellets.

pg. 278

gills
scales
school
fins and tail
other fish or smaller sea creatures

pg. 279

(Some answers may vary)
1. rattlesnakes
2. cobras
1. When an alligator's mouth is closed, you can see only its top teeth. When a crocodile's mouth is closed, you can see all of its teeth.
2. A crocodile's snout is wider than an alligator's.
3. Alligators are found mostly in the southeastern United States, whereas crocodiles are found on almost every continent.

pg. 280

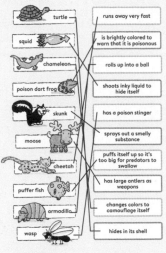

giraffe, cheetah, parrot, whale, deer, shark, octopus, woodpecker, buffalo, squirrel, toucan, zebra

WOODLAND
RAIN FOREST
GRASSLAND
OCEAN

pg. 281

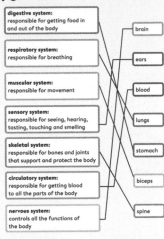

turtle — hides in its shell
squid — shoots inky liquid to hide itself
chameleon — changes colors to camouflage itself
poison dart frog — is brightly colored to warn that it is poisonous
skunk — sprays out a smelly substance
moose — has large antlers as weapons
cheetah — runs away very fast
puffer fish — puffs itself up so it's too big for predators to swallow
armadilla — rolls up into a ball
wasp — has a poison stinger

pg. 282

digestive system: responsible for getting food in and out of the body
respiratory system: responsible for breathing
muscular system: responsible for movement
sensory system: responsible for seeing, hearing, tasting, touching and smelling
skeletal system: responsible for bones and joints that support and protect the body
circulatory system: responsible for getting blood to all the parts of the body
nervous system: controls all the functions of the body

brain, ears, blood, lungs, stomach, biceps, spine

pg. 283

206
103
the brain
ligaments
calcium

pg. 284

balanced
unbalanced
table
tower
gravity

pg. 285

balanced
unbalanced
balanced
unbalanced
balanced
unbalanced

pg. 286

Tuesday
Sunday, Thursday, Saturday
Tuesday
Sunday
Friday

pg. 288

pull together
push apart
M: paper clip, safety pin, nail, bolt, metal spoon

TECHNOLOGY

pg. 290

Dear Janita,
How are ~~Howare~~ you I am practicing typing. I ~~hhhope~~ hope you have a good day today!

Your friend,
Petra

pg. 291

I_L0ve_2C0d3
C@tsAr3C00l!
Bra1n@Qu3st21

pg. 292

pg. 293

pg. 294

(sample answer)
Loop [Go 1] 5 times
Turn Right
Go Forward 1
Go Forward 1
Turn Left
Loop [Go 1] 5 times
Turn Left
Loop [Go 1] 2 times

pg. 295

Go Forward 1
Turn Right
Loop [Go 1] 2 times
Turn Left
Loop [Go 1] 8 times
Turn Left
Loop [Go 1] 2 times
Turn Left
Loop [Go 1] 3 times

pg. 296

Go Forward 1
If seal, then turn left
Go Forward 1
Go Forward 1
Go Forward 1

pg. 297

Loop [GO 1] 2 times
If seal, then turn left
Loop [GO 1] 2 times
If orca, then turn left
Loop [GO 1] 2 times

pg. 299

7
5
2
go online

pg. 300

Can you read this?

BRAIN QUEST EXTRAS

You did it! Time to make a Brain Quest Mini-Deck so you can play and learn wherever you go. Fill out your certificate and hang your poster. Great work!

PARENTS Congratulations to you and your child. In this section your child can cut out the Brain Quest Mini-Deck and certificate and hang up their poster. Continue to make learning part of your everyday life beyond this book. Keep reading with your child, guide them to see the math in everyday life, and ask questions to help encourage their curiosity and extend their learning.

CONGRATULATIONS!

You've finished the Brain Quest Workbook!

All your hard work paid off! Cut out these Brain Quest Smart Cards to make your own Mini-Deck.

You can play these anywhere—in the back of the car, at the park, or even at the grocery store. Remember: It's fun to be smart!®

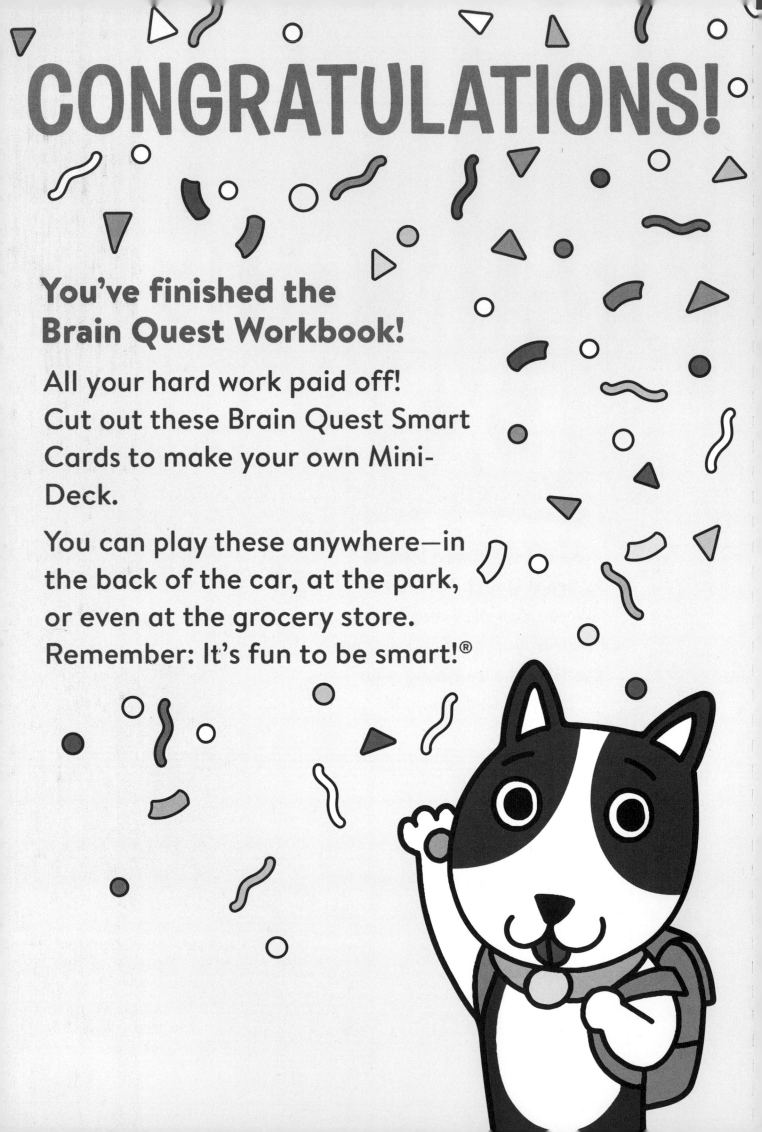

QUESTIONS

 MATH What is the sum of 858 and 167?

 LANGUAGE ARTS Put the number words in alphabetical order: <u>thirteen</u>, <u>third</u>, <u>three</u>

 MATH Change this to a multiplication problem: $5 + 5 + 5 + 5 + 5 + 5 = 30$

 LANGUAGE ARTS Spell the five-letter word that means the opposite of *here*.

BRAIN QUEST

QUESTIONS

 MATH What's the sum of 224 and 551?

 MISCELLANY What do we call a person who mends clothes for a living?

 MATH Sophie has 20 buttons. Each shirt needs 6. How many shirts can she make?

 LANGUAGE ARTS Spell the name of the joint between the thigh and the calf that rhymes with *pea*.

BRAIN QUEST

QUESTIONS

 MATH $9 + 3 = 15 - 4$ True or false?

 LANGUAGE ARTS Spell the plural of *witch*.

 MATH What is the denominator in $6\frac{4}{8}$?

 READING Which should be written as one word: <u>finger nail</u> or <u>finger puppet</u>?

BRAIN QUEST

QUESTIONS

 MATH The numerator is the top number of a fraction. What is the bottom number called?

 LANGUAGE ARTS Correct this sentence: "Your the brightest bulb in the box."

 MATH In the division problem $36 \div 4 = 9$, what is the name for the number 9?

 READING Which is a synonym of *interested*: <u>uncertain</u>, <u>curious</u>, <u>talkative</u>?

BRAIN QUEST

QUESTIONS

 MATH How many ounces are in a pint?

 LANGUAGE ARTS How do you spell the plural of knife?

 MISCELLANY In baseball, is home plate shaped like a <u>hexagon</u> or a <u>pentagon</u>?

 READING Change the verb to its past form: "The dog begins to howl."

BRAIN QUEST

QUESTIONS

 MATH Round $762.32 to the nearest hundred dollars.

 READING "Dorothy followed the yellow brick road." What pronouns can replace the subject?

 MATH Is the difference between 129 and 98 <u>greater than</u> or <u>less than</u> 30?

 LANGUAGE ARTS What letters do *cantaloupe* and *celebration* have in common?

BRAIN QUEST

Brain Quest Mini-Deck

Card 1

ANSWERS

MATH 1 2 3

False (9 + 3 = 12 and 15 − 4 = 11)

LANGUAGE ARTS A B C

w–i–t–c–h–e–s (witches)

MATH 1 2 3

8

READING

fingernail

BRAIN QUEST

Card 2

ANSWERS

MATH 1 2 3

775 (224 + 551 = 775)

MISCELLANY ?

a tailor or seamstress

MATH 1 2 3

3 shirts (with 2 buttons left over)

LANGUAGE ARTS A B C

k–n–e–e (knee)

BRAIN QUEST

Card 3

ANSWERS

MATH 1 2 3

1,025 (858 + 167 = 1,025)

LANGUAGE ARTS A B C

third, thirteen, three

MATH 1 2 3

6 × 5 = 30

LANGUAGE ARTS A B C

t–h–e–r–e (there)

BRAIN QUEST

Card 4

ANSWERS

MATH 1 2 3

$800.00

READING

She, They

MATH 1 2 3

less than (127 − 98 = 29)

LANGUAGE ARTS A B C

c, a, n, t, l, o, e

BRAIN QUEST

Card 5

ANSWERS

MATH 1 2 3

16 ounces

LANGUAGE ARTS A B C

k–n–i–v–e–s (knives)

MISCELLANY ?

a pentagon

READING

"The dog began to howl."

BRAIN QUEST

Card 6

ANSWERS

MATH 1 2 3

the denominator

LANGUAGE ARTS A B C

"You're the brightest bulb in the box."

MATH 1 2 3

the quotient (the answer)

READING

curious

BRAIN QUEST

Brain Quest Mini-Deck

QUESTIONS

 MATH The fractions $\frac{1}{6}$, $\frac{5}{30}$, and $\frac{2}{12}$ are all equal. True or false?

 MISCELLANY Is a botanist someone who studies <u>bugs</u> or <u>plants</u>?

 MATH Which of these numbers is a mixed fraction: $\frac{12}{4}$ or $2\frac{1}{3}$?

 READING Find the adjective in this sentence: "The forgetful man left his newspaper at the diner."

BRAIN QUEST®

QUESTIONS

 MATH Jonas has 400 pieces of paper. He uses 320 for his novel. How many are left for his short stories?

 READING Correct the tense of the verb: "Our class saw the movie tomorrow."

 MATH How many hundreds equal 1,000?

 READING When abbreviating the date, does the month come <u>before</u> or <u>after</u> the day?

BRAIN QUEST®

QUESTIONS

 MATH Put the fractions in order from greatest to least: $\frac{5}{8}$, $\frac{5}{6}$, $\frac{5}{7}$

 LANGUAGE ARTS Spell the number that is one less than fourteen.

 MISCELLANY When it is 6:20, where is the minute hand on a clock?

 READING Use two of these words to make a compound word: <u>time</u>, <u>arrow</u>, <u>night</u>, <u>pole</u>

BRAIN QUEST®

QUESTIONS

 MATH What number is 5 less than the sum of 6 and 4?

 READING What is the root word in this word group: <u>electricity</u>, <u>electrician</u>, <u>electrical</u>?

 MATH How many inches are in 4 feet?

 MISCELLANY Which animals live in the ocean: <u>orcas</u>, <u>orangutans</u>, <u>snakes</u>, <u>porcupines</u>?

BRAIN QUEST®

QUESTIONS

 MATH There are 5 oranges and 3 apples in a bowl. What fraction of the fruit is apples?

 MISCELLANY What kind of reference book gives information on many different topics?

 MATH We were winning 5–2. Then they scored 4 points. How many points did we need to tie the game?

 READING "Wash your hands before dinner." Is this sentence a <u>question</u> or a <u>command</u>?

BRAIN QUEST®

QUESTIONS

 MATH Say the next three numbers in this series: 350, 300, 250, 200, . . .

 LANGUAGE ARTS Spell the contraction of *who is*.

 MATH How much is 9×9?

 LANGUAGE ARTS What is the correct spelling of the past tense of pay: p–a–y–e–d or p–a–i–d?

BRAIN QUEST®

Brain Quest Mini-Deck

Card 1

ANSWERS

MATH 1 2 3

$\frac{5}{6}, \frac{5}{7}, \frac{5}{8}$

LANGUAGE ARTS A B C

t–h–i–r–t–e–e–n (thirteen)

MISCELLANY ?

on the 4

READING

nighttime (night + time)

BRAIN QUEST

Card 2

ANSWERS

MATH 1 2 3

80 pieces of paper (420 – 300 = 80)

READING

"Our class will see the movie tomorrow."

MATH 1 2 3

10 hundreds (10 x 100 = 1,000)

READING

before

BRAIN QUEST

Card 3

ANSWERS

MATH 1 2 3

true

MISCELLANY ?

plants

MATH 1 2 3

$2\frac{1}{3}$

READING

"The forgetful man left his newspaper at the diner."

BRAIN QUEST

Card 4

ANSWERS

MATH 1 2 3

150, 100, 50

LANGUAGE ARTS A B C

w–h–o–'–s (who's)

MATH 1 2 3

81

LANGUAGE ARTS A B C

p–a–i–d (paid)

BRAIN QUEST

Card 5

ANSWERS

MATH 1 2 3

$\frac{3}{8}$

MISCELLANY ?

an encyclopedia

MATH 1 2 3

1 point

READING

a command

BRAIN QUEST

Card 6

ANSWERS

MATH 1 2 3

5 (6 + 4 = 10; 10 – 5 = 5)

READING

electric

MATH 1 2 3

48 inches (4 × 12 = 48)

MISCELLANY ?

orcas

BRAIN QUEST

Brain Quest Mini-Deck

QUESTIONS

 MATH We bought 32 toffee bits and used $\frac{1}{4}$ of them in our cookies. How many toffee bits did we use?

 LANGUAGE ARTS Spell the name of the day that follows Monday.

 MATH If you add two odd numbers, is the answer <u>odd</u> or <u>even</u>?

READING Which is not a synonym of *calm*: <u>peaceful</u>, <u>cheerful</u>, <u>restful</u>?

BRAIN QUEST

QUESTIONS

 MATH How many corners are on a cube?

 MISCELLANY ? What is the name for someone who designs houses?

 MATH How many odd numbers are there between 14 and 26?

 READING Identify the two consonants: <u>w</u>, <u>u</u>, <u>i</u>, <u>y</u>, <u>e</u>

BRAIN QUEST

QUESTIONS

 MATH How many angles are in a triangle?

 LANGUAGE ARTS What is the correct spelling: h–i–w–a–y or h–i–g–h–w–a–y?

 MATH There are 50 people in line. 22 people are behind Nell. How many are in front of her?

 MISCELLANY ? When you don't have any responsibilities, do you feel <u>careful</u> or <u>carefree</u>?

BRAIN QUEST

QUESTIONS

 MATH What is the name of the period in the number 3.24?

 LANGUAGE ARTS Which words should be capitalized? "no one wants sam to move to new mexico."

 MATH Which fraction is equivalent to $\frac{1}{3}$: $\frac{3}{9}$ or $\frac{2}{12}$?

 READING Divide the word *coffee* into syllables.

BRAIN QUEST

QUESTIONS

 MATH In a group of 100 students, half are third graders and half are fourth graders. How many are in each grade?

 LANGUAGE ARTS Which fruit comes first in the dictionary: <u>apple</u> or <u>apricot</u>?

 MATH What's the best estimate for the length of a soup spoon: <u>half a foot</u> or <u>20 inches</u>?

 READING What punctuation usually follows the words *how* and *what*?

BRAIN QUEST

QUESTIONS

 MISCELLANY ? Is 12 a.m. at <u>midnight</u> or <u>midday</u>?

 READING Say this sentence in the present tense: "My mom weighed the grapes on the scale."

 MATH What are the next two numbers in the series 2, 4, 8, 16?

 READING Make the nouns in this sentence singular: "Put the fishes back in the tanks."

BRAIN QUEST

Brain Quest Mini-Deck

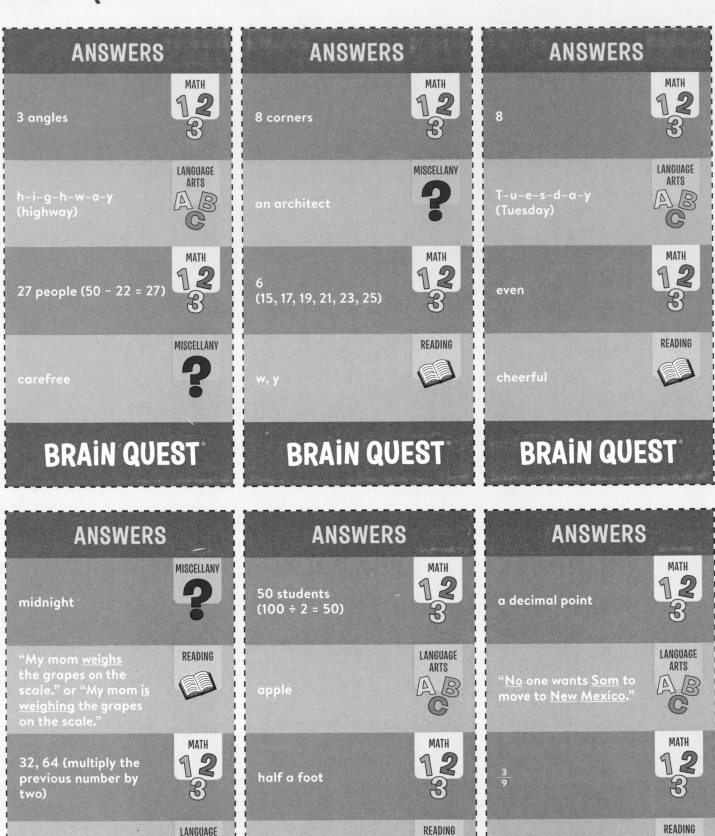

ANSWERS

MATH 1 2 3
3 angles

LANGUAGE ARTS A B C
h–i–g–h–w–a–y (highway)

MATH 1 2 3
27 people (50 – 22 = 27)

MISCELLANY ?
carefree

BRAIN QUEST

ANSWERS

MATH 1 2 3
8 corners

MISCELLANY ?
an architect

MATH 1 2 3
6
(15, 17, 19, 21, 23, 25)

READING
w, y

BRAIN QUEST

ANSWERS

MATH 1 2 3
8

LANGUAGE ARTS A B C
T–u–e–s–d–a–y (Tuesday)

MATH 1 2 3
even

READING
cheerful

BRAIN QUEST

ANSWERS

MISCELLANY ?
midnight

READING
"My mom weighs the grapes on the scale." or "My mom is weighing the grapes on the scale."

MATH 1 2 3
32, 64 (multiply the previous number by two)

LANGUAGE ARTS A B C
"Put the fish back in the tank."

BRAIN QUEST

ANSWERS

MATH 1 2 3
50 students
(100 ÷ 2 = 50)

LANGUAGE ARTS A B C
apple

MATH 1 2 3
half a foot

READING
a question mark

BRAIN QUEST

ANSWERS

MATH 1 2 3
a decimal point

LANGUAGE ARTS A B C
"No one wants Sam to move to New Mexico."

MATH 1 2 3
$\frac{3}{9}$

READING
cof • fee

BRAIN QUEST

Brain Quest Mini-Deck

QUESTIONS

 MATH What is the product of 42 × 0?

 READING The word *ad* is short for what goes on a billboard. What is the full word?

 MATH How many minutes are in a quarter of an hour?

READING "My mom and her partners made a business deal." What is the complete subject of this sentence?

BRAIN QUEST

QUESTIONS

 MATH How many quarters are in $3.00?

 LANGUAGE ARTS Is the past tense of the word "hear" spelled h–e–r–d or h–e–a–r–d?

 MATH If the carnival is in town for 6 weeks, how many weekend days will the carnival be in town?

READING What word in a name is abbreviated D–r–period?

BRAIN QUEST

QUESTIONS

 MATH The Putras started driving at 11:30 a.m. and arrived at 1:15 p.m. How long was the car ride?

 MISCELLANY ? Which is the opposite of *broader*: <u>narrower</u> or <u>nearer</u>?

 MATH Change $\frac{7}{10}$ to a decimal.

READING Rearrange the letters in *ward* to find a word that means *to sketch*.

BRAIN QUEST

QUESTIONS

 MATH How do you write the fraction seven-eighths: <u>8 over 7</u> or <u>7 over 8</u>?

 READING Does *exaggerate* mean to <u>overstate untruthfully</u> or to <u>explode suddenly</u>?

 MATH What is another way to write $\frac{3}{3}$?

 MISCELLANY ? *Ship* is to *sea* as *train* is to _____?

BRAIN QUEST

QUESTIONS

 MATH How much is 38 – 7 – 10 – 1?

 LANGUAGE ARTS If you step on a scale, will you learn how much you w–h–e–y or how much you w–e–i–g–h?

 MATH Which is biggest: 1 half gallon, 1 pint, or 1 quart?

 LANGUAGE ARTS Take two letters away from *fiend* to make a word for a shark's body part.

BRAIN QUEST

QUESTIONS

 MATH Subtract 305 from 526.

 READING What letter is not pronounced in the word *hasten*?

 MATH How many seconds are there in $3\frac{1}{2}$ minutes?

 READING Find the antonyms: "Maisie was present, but Luke and Angga were absent."

BRAIN QUEST

Brain Quest Mini-Deck

ANSWERS

MATH 1 2 3
1 hour 45 minutes

MISCELLANY ?
narrower

MATH 1 2 3
0.7

READING
draw

BRAIN QUEST®

ANSWERS

LANGUAGE ARTS A B C
12 quarters

LANGUAGE ARTS A B C
h–e–a–r–d (heard)

MATH 1 2 3
12 days (2 x 6 = 12)

MISCELLANY ?
Doctor (for example, Dr. Johnson)

BRAIN QUEST®

ANSWERS

MATH 1 2 3
0 (Any number multiplied by 0 equals 0.)

READING
advertisement

MATH 1 2 3
15 minutes

READING
"My mom and her partners made a business deal."

BRAIN QUEST®

ANSWERS

MATH 1 2 3
221 (526 – 305 = 221)

READING
the t (has ten)

MATH 1 2 3
210 (60 + 60 + 60 + 30)

READING
"Maisie was present, but Luke and Angga were absent."

BRAIN QUEST®

ANSWERS

MATH 1 2 3
20

LANGUAGE ARTS A B C
w–e–i–g–h (weigh)

MISCELLANY ?
1 half gallon (equals 2 quarts or 4 pints)

LANGUAGE ARTS A B C
fin (take away e and d)

BRAIN QUEST®

ANSWERS

MATH 1 2 3
7 over 8 ($\frac{7}{8}$)

READING
to overstate untruthfully

MATH 1 2 3
1 (3 ÷ 3 = 1)

MISCELLANY ?
tracks

BRAIN QUEST®

YOU DID IT!

CONGRATULATIONS!

You completed every activity in the Brain Quest Grade 3 Workbook. Cut out the certificate and write your name on it. Show your friends! Hang it on the wall! You should feel proud of your hard work.

CERTIFICATE OF
ACHIEVEMENT

Earned by

_____

for completing all sections in the

BRAIN QUEST®
GRADE 3 WORKBOOK